SENSATIONAL
EDNA ANDRADE'S DRAWINGS

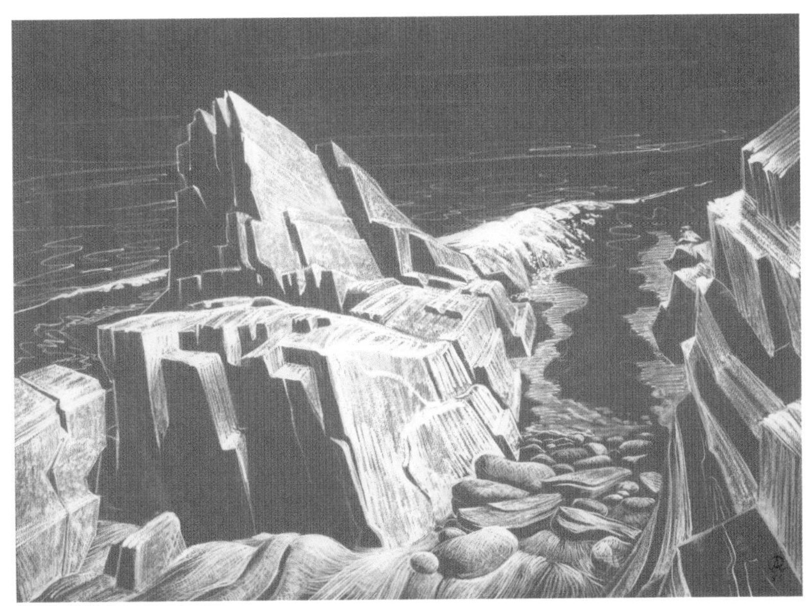

Woodmere Art Museum

March 25 – June 24, 2007

Lenders to the Exhibition

Linda Lee Alter
Michael Basta
Mrs. Nida Bernstein and Todd Bernstein
Thomas A. Bershad
Luther W. Brady
Bryn Mawr College
Theodore and Nancie Burkett
Diane Burko and Richard Ryan
Jessica Burko
Julie and Neil Courtney
Dr. Janice T. Gordon
Ann and Donald McPhail
Elizabeth Osborne
Pennsylvania Academy of the Fine Arts
Portia Sperr
Essie and Steve Springer
Mr. and Mrs. James B. Straw
Edna Andrade and Locks Gallery
and a private collector

Sensational: Edna Andrade's Drawings was curated by W. Douglass Paschall.

The exhibition catalogue was designed by Sosson Design.

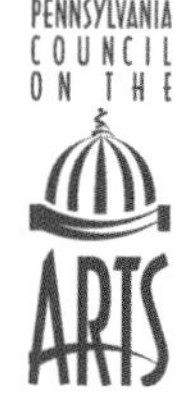

Woodmere Art Museum receives arts funding support through grants from the Pennsylvania Council on the Arts (a state agency) and the Philadelphia Cultural Fund.

Corporate Sponsors

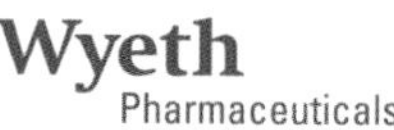

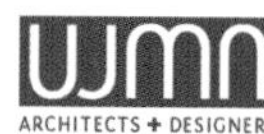

Media Sponsor

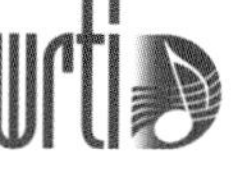

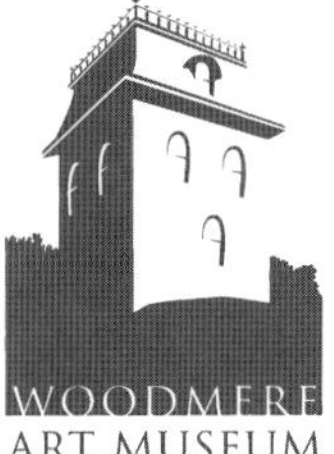

Celebrating Philadelphia's Artistic Legacy

ISBN 1-888008-19-9

Foreword

With the exhibition *Sensational: Edna Andrade's Drawings*, Woodmere Art Museum is honored to acknowledge the genius of one of Philadelphia's most treasured artists on the occasion of her ninetieth birthday. Moreover, it pleases me to note that the act of featuring the art of senior artists is far from unprecedented at Woodmere. I remember fondly, for instance, the exhibits assembled in similar fashion to celebrate the artistic contributions of Arthur Meltzer and Paulette van Roekens on the occasion of their ninetieth birthdays, and exhibits mounted for other veteran artists such as John Lear and Bill Campbell. All of these artists, like Edna Andrade, pursued their art with the verve and alacrity of youth. Although Andrade's art has been the subject of innumerable exhibitions over the years, it seems remarkable that no extensive array of her drawings has been mounted before now. Woodmere Art Museum's Curator of Collections, W. Douglass Paschall, has gone a long way in filling that void by assembling a comprehensive, evolutionary look at this little-explored facet of Edna Andrade's illustrious career, and his informative essay in this catalogue adds fresh analysis to the interpretation of her incomparable contributions to the art of our time.

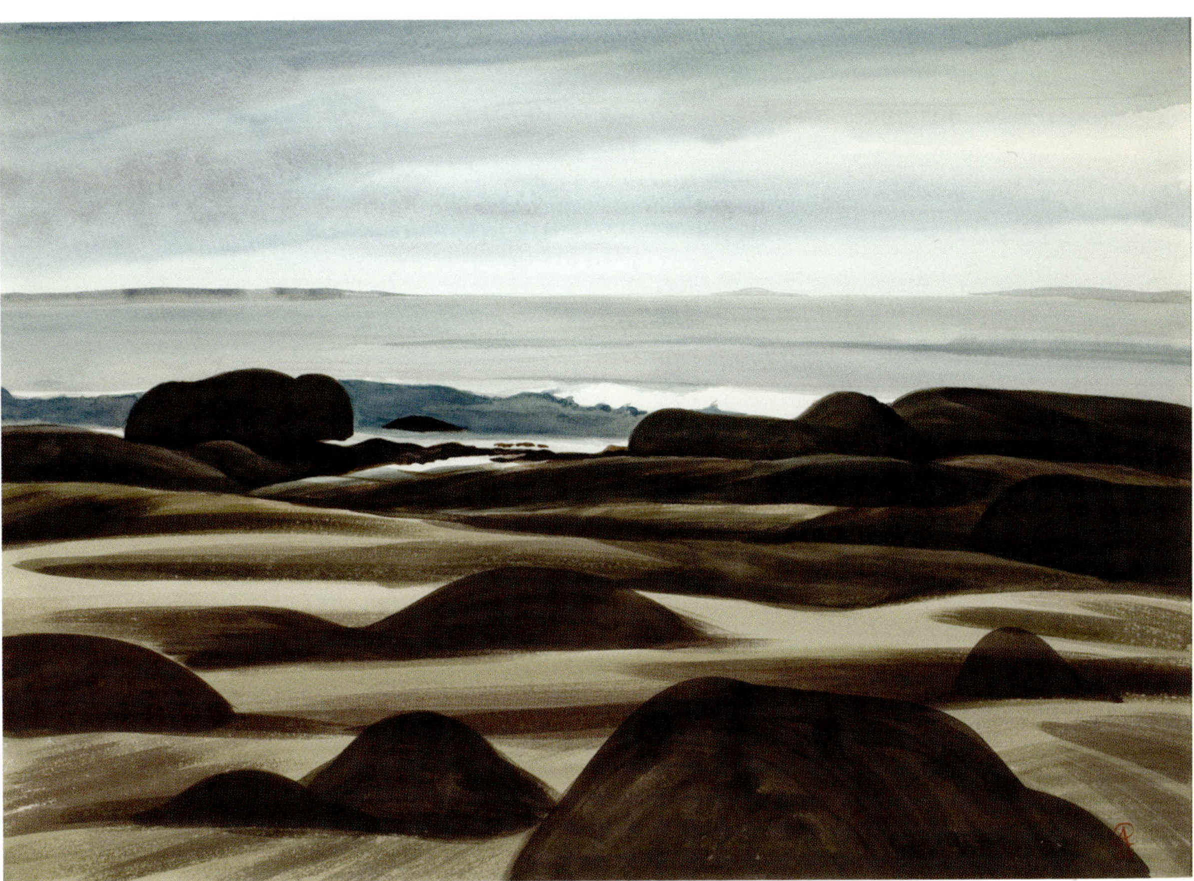

Black Rocks, 1953, cat. 3

This tribute is made possible by a wonderful outpouring of financial support from many different individuals and corporations, including a generous leadership gift from Wyeth Pharmaceuticals. To the following additional sponsors we also extend profound gratitude: Lee Alter and Seymour Mednick, Elie-Antoine Atallah, A.I.A, The Helen Bershad Foundation, Dr. Susan H. Bray, Peter F. Cooke, Jr., Jay Eshleman, D.D.S., Lawrence Finkelstein, Esq., Dr. Abraham Freedman, Vivian A. A. Gast, Howard T. Hallowell III, Ralph S. Hirshorn, Patrick J. Hoyer, Charles J. Ingersoll, Dr. Robert Kalish, Marguerite Lenfest, Frannie and Jim Maguire, The Maguire Foundation, Donald and Ann McPhail, Dianne A. Meyer, Esq., Gary G. Miller, Joseph A. Nicholson, A.I.A., I.D.S.A., The Pennsylvania Council on the Arts, The Philadelphia Cultural Fund, Ned and Kathy Putnam, the Schantz family, Mr. and Mrs. Edwin Sherman, Charles E. Sigety, Esq., UJMN Architects + Designers, Mary Ann B. Wirts, and Joseph M. Yohlin, Esq.

Naturally, we are equally grateful to the many lenders, listed at left, who so willingly shared their artistic treasures to make this important retrospective possible.

Michael W. Schantz, Ph.D.
The Patricia Van Burgh Allison Director & CEO

Acknowledgments

The current exhibition, the first in a museum to cover Edna Andrade's full career, owes its existence to many individuals and organizations. At the outset, the vital archival research to shed light on lesser-known periods of the artist's life and training was made both possible and immensely pleasurable with the indispensable assistance of Judy Throm and Marisa Bourgoin of the Archives of American Art/Smithsonian Institution; Cheryl Leibold and the library staff of the Pennsylvania Academy of the Fine Arts; Sara MacDonald, Regina Barthmaier, Jennifer Edwards, and Steve Tarantal of the University of the Arts; Richard Torchia of Arcadia University; Sarah Biemiller of The Print Center of Philadelphia; Amey Hutchins of the University of Pennsylvania; Lisa Hancock of the Virginia Museum of Fine Arts; and Erin Lopater of the Chrysler Museum of Art. Conversations and correspondence with Andrade's generous colleagues, admirers, and friends William White, Leonard Lehrer, Elizabeth Osborne, Diane Burko, Burt Wasserman, and Victoria Donohoe added firsthand personal accounts to put vivid flesh on the bare bones of the documentary evidence.

As we next sought pivotal artworks to represent the many phases of Andrade's remarkable career in the Museum's galleries and exhibition catalogue, the unflinching generosity of Carol Campbell and Tamara Johnston of the Bryn Mawr College Art and Archaeology Collections; Kim Sajet, Alex Baker, and Robert Harmon of the Pennsylvania Academy of the Fine Arts; and many private collectors of the artist's drawings, collages, and paintings proved to us how profound and how deeply appreciated the impact has been that this artist continues to exert on the Philadelphia area's contemporary art scene.

Anyone interested in Andrade's works invariably relies on the tireless enthusiasm and aid of the Locks Gallery, her dealer of thirty-five years, its director, Sueyun Locks, and staff members Philip Mott, Joseph Hu, and, above all, Doug Schaller, who pulled out all the stops to open the gallery's research files, steer us to collectors, arrange loans of works still in the artist's possession, and introduce us to the warm circle of Andrade's devoted admirers.

Finally, we owe our deepest debt of gratitude to Edna Andrade herself, who patiently and graciously answered every question, cleared up every error, opened every storage drawer, and dug out every carefully saved document or photograph with the feisty warmth and good-humored charm that are her trademarks, and who more importantly over six decades as an artist, in countless re-imaginings, has produced the marvels that would conjure us to see.

W. Douglass Paschall
Curator of Collections

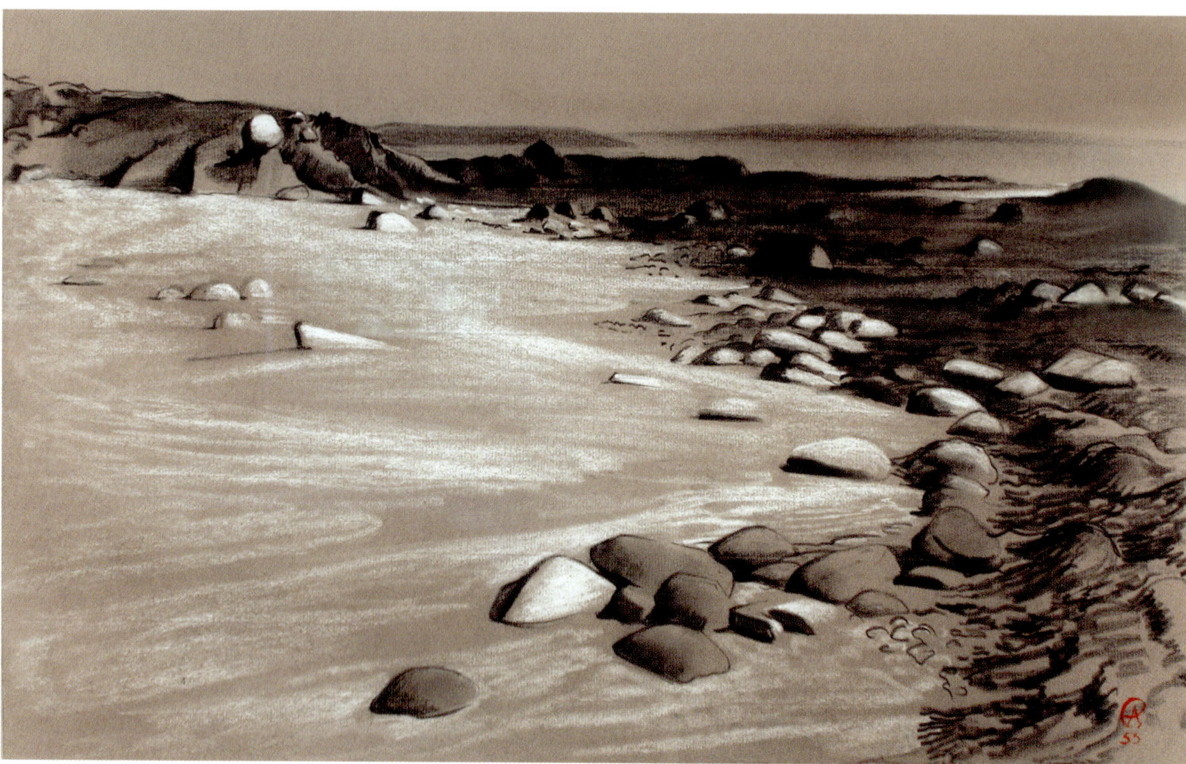

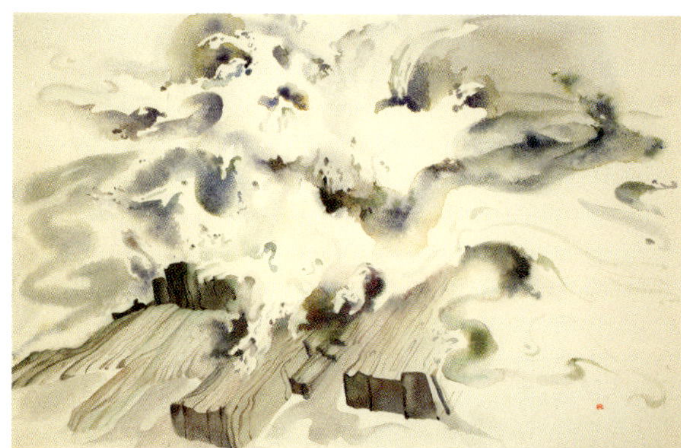

Top: *Distant White Boulder*, 1953, cat. 5
Below: *Breaking Wave*, 1953, cat. 4

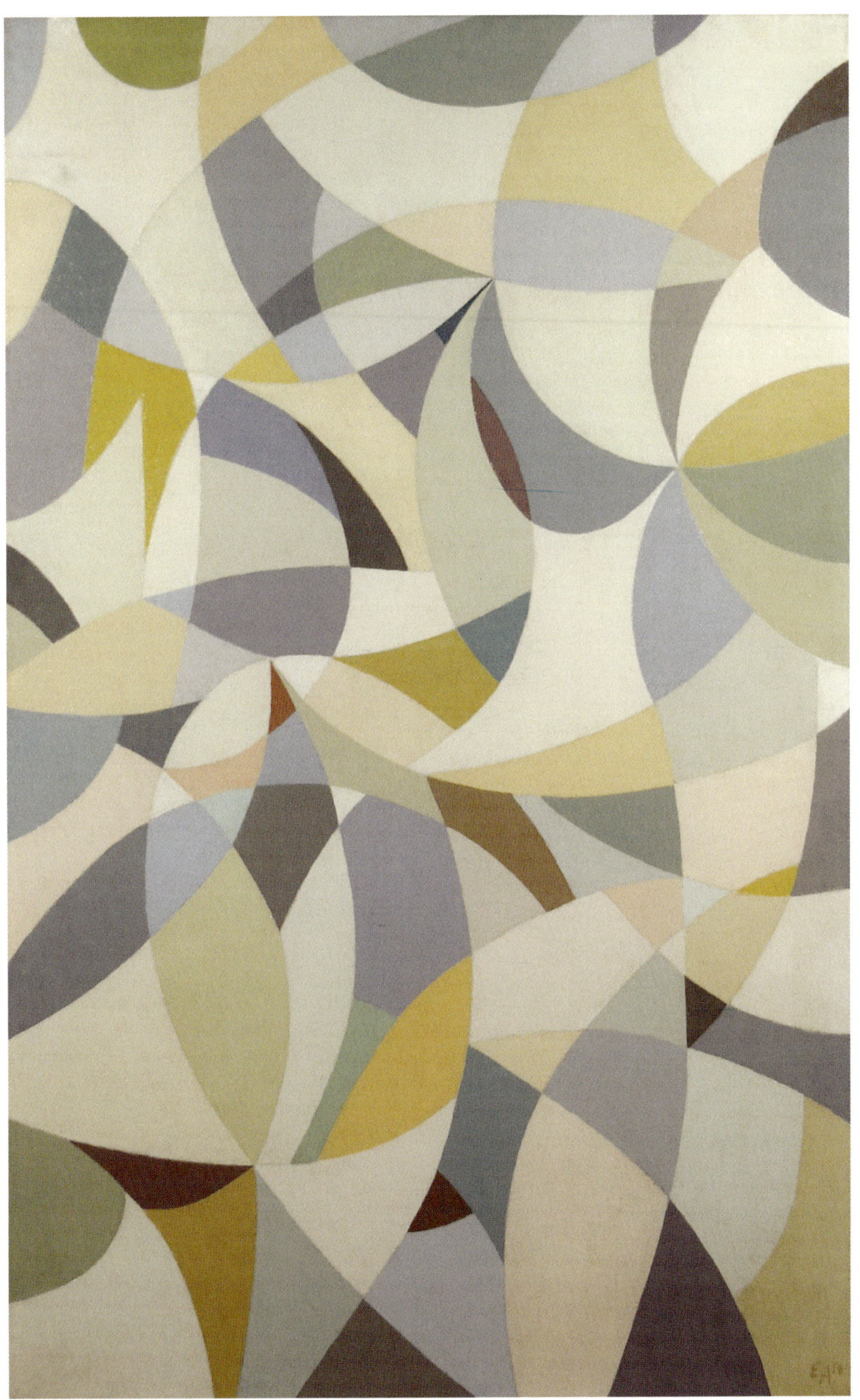

Flight of Gulls, 1958, cat. 8

The Romantic Geometer

by W. Douglass Paschall

At the age of ninety, Edna Andrade is at once one of the most renowned of Philadelphia's artists and yet still a bit of a cipher.[1] Her geometric paintings from the 1960s headline major museum exhibitions of the Op Art movement, now undergoing a resurgence of interest, at the same time as her more recent works, meticulous in their representation of the weathered rocks of the Maine coastline, garner consistent critical praise and collector attention. That two such impulses, on the surface so far apart in ambitions, could stem from a single aesthetic sensibility has made it difficult to cast the artist's career and stylistic development in a convenient, linear storyline. Two institutions, the Pennsylvania Academy of the Fine Arts and the Institute of Contemporary Art in Philadelphia, that mounted retrospective exhibitions of Andrade's works in 1993 and 2003, chose to narrow their focus to the geometric works with which she first gained a large national audience. Even then, to characterize what is most distinctive about those pieces, the essayists for those exhibitions' catalogues dwelt as much on what they are not as on what they are.[2] This is an artist who has eluded easy description.

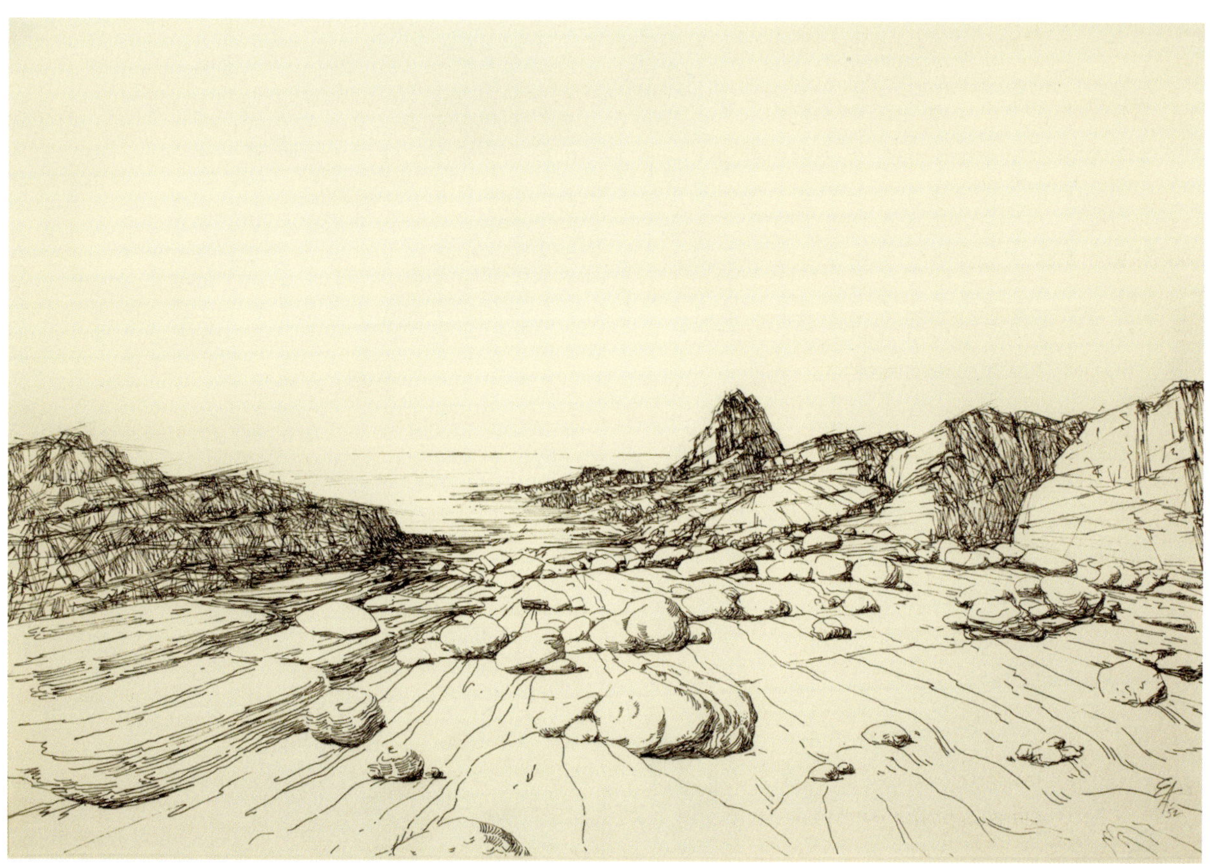

Bailey Island, 1952, cat. 2

Part of the challenge lies precisely in the artist's age. Andrade is almost a full generation older than many of the artists with whom she has been stylistically associated. Her training and the philosophical, social, and artistic agendas that she has embraced are of an earlier phase of modern cultural inquiry. To have been productive for more than six decades, moreover, has given Andrade the arc of time to evolve, and evolve again, as few of her confreres did. This span gives us today an opportunity to look over the full (or near-full) trajectory of the artist's career to discern the threads that have been consistent throughout.

Andrade, like many of the first-generation modernist artists she admires, had a traditional education in art. Growing up in the countryside of Tidewater Virginia, amid the rampant natural abundance of the Great Dismal Swamp, Edna Wright (her maiden name) undertook her first art lessons in classes organized by Pennsylvania Academy graduate Glenna Latimer. The recommendation of her teacher earned the promising student admittance to the Pennsylvania Academy, one of the most prestigious and demanding, albeit conservative, schools in the nation. In painting classes led by the Impressionist Daniel Garber, she concentrated on landscape subjects. Another teacher, Henry McCarter, introduced her to European modernism and encouraged her to take additional classes at the Barnes Foundation. In her final year at the Academy, in a class conducted by George Harding, she specialized in mural painting, earning a Cresson Traveling Scholarship for a social-realist mural depicting the busy interior of her father's Virginia sawmill.

Andrade's training exposed her to the divergent paths that were open to young artists in the 1930s, stressing representational styles (which, aside from anyone's aesthetic preferences, had the marked advantage of being more saleable in the depths of

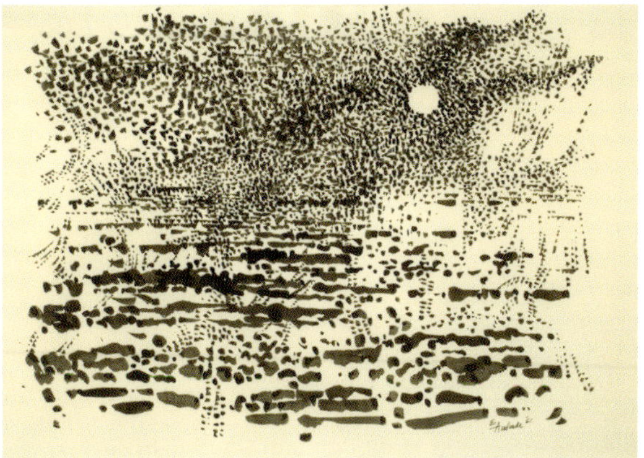

Moon Rise, 1961, cat. 9

the Depression) but also admitting the spur of more progressive modes of art. The Academy, too, almost as much as its rival, the Pennsylvania Museum School of Industrial Art, at this time downplayed the division between high and low art, between the self-consciously purist notion of creating masterpieces for museums and the practical consideration of earning a living supplying imagery to the commercial and civic entities that were rebuilding a struggling economy. Bridging both realms was a career as a teacher.

Following travels in Europe on her Cresson Scholarship, Andrade returned to Virginia, taking a position leading art programs in the public schools of Norfolk and devouring books on the pedagogy of art. In a subsequent two-year appointment teaching at the H. Sophie Newcomb Memorial College in New Orleans, she met Robert Durant Feild, who began replacing that school's Beaux-Arts curriculum with new methods of instruction from the German Bauhaus that emphasized the formal building blocks of image-making, experiments in perception, and technical mastery of modern industrial materials.[3]

The transformation that might have been anticipated at this moment, when the young artist was among the first in this country to experience first-hand a wholly novel conception of the nature and function of art, would be postponed. In the summer of 1941 she married Preston Andrade, a young architect in Philadelphia, and only months later the couple moved to Washington, D.C., with the outbreak of the Second World War. Edna Andrade found employment in the Visual Presentation Division of the Office of Strategic Services, working with Eero Saarinen, John Ford, and Disney Studio animators to design and produce instructional materials for the war effort. As the war continued, she and several other designers left the O.S.S. to form their own cooperative, creating posters, charts, and films for the Treasury Department and labor unions.

In 1946 the Andrades returned to Philadelphia to re-establish civilian careers. Edna helped out as a draughtsman in her husband's architectural firm and took a commission for a mural for the Asiatic Hall of the Academy of Natural Sciences of Philadelphia, leaving her little time to pursue her own painting. In 1950, when Preston Andrade took another architectural posting in New York, the couple moved to Bucks County, settling into a house across the road from her former teacher Daniel Garber's Cuttalossa farm. The exile from concerted art-making that inevitably accompanied these repeated moves was not unusual, the artist concedes: "A lot of people in my generation went through the hiatus of the war, which literally took ten years out of your life."[4] When

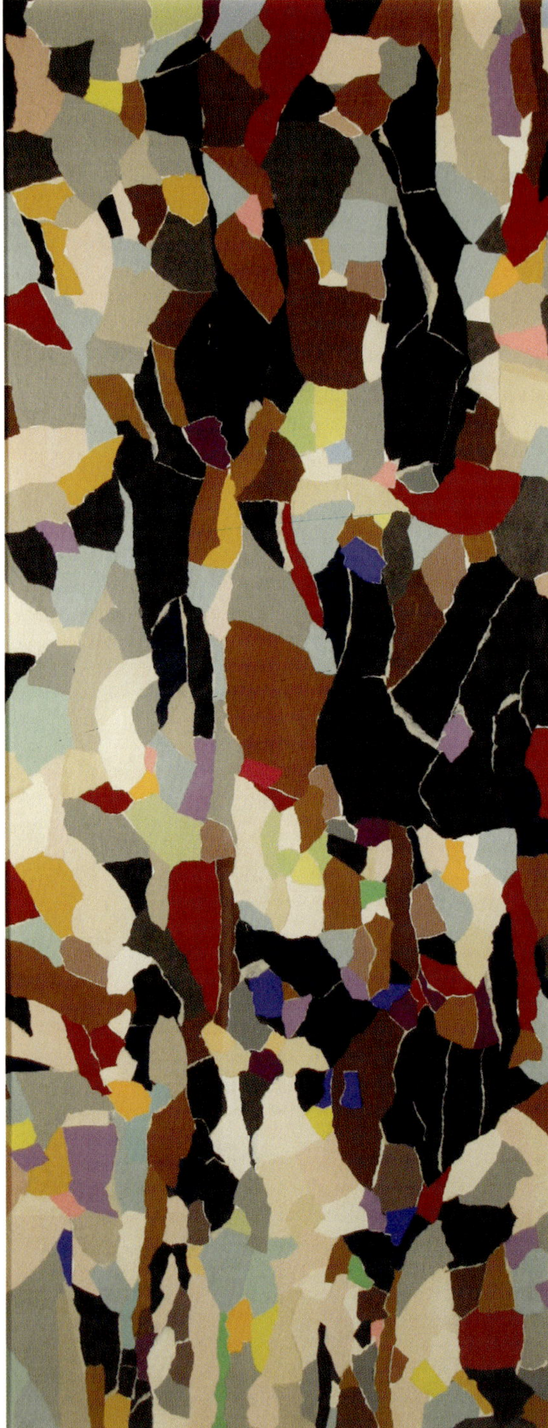

Dark Figures, 1962, cat. 10

at last she was able to wrest time to embark on a personal creative output, she did so in a context much altered from the 1930s.

The presence of European artists in New York during the war and exhibitions at that city's Art of This Century and Julien Levy Galleries initiated a vogue for Surrealism — and notoriety for an American offshoot, the Abstract Expressionists — that dominated the progressive art press of the late 1940s and early 1950s and the developing styles of artists across the nation. As Andrade sought her own voice in this new firmament, "I was doing a kind of 'magic realism' at that time and the work was organized around a tonal system of darks and lights."[5] It was these playful scenes of circus performers or moody paintings of bathers isolated on deserted beaches, sometimes "collaged" with discordant symbolic elements from the natural world, that Andrade began to submit to exhibitions, along with mobile sculptures that, though representational, gave outlet to some of the formal preoccupations she had absorbed from exposure to Bauhaus theories.

At the same time, mostly on summer vacations in Maine, she pursued a quite different set of challenges in a number of drawings and watercolors of the New England coast. Drawings have long been a way for artists to "keep their hands in," at once a welcome respite from the unitary focus of painting or sculpting, an opportunity to take up or return to alternative subjects, and a chance to reconnect at the most elemental, physical level with the manual discipline of representation. Drawings also provide the most immediate and conveniently mobile means to explore new ideas and solutions, and it was this aspect that (we can see in retrospect) would lead Andrade farthest in her personal artistic growth through the remainder of the decade. Alternating among ink, charcoal, pastel, gouache, and watercolor media, Andrade used these renderings of the rugged Maine shoreline to examine and test structure: the physical structure of the eroded rocks she was depicting and the pictorial structure of lights and darks that would define her compositions. Though determinedly representational, these dramatic works were anything but the calm, idyllic landscapes her Bucks County neighbors were creating.

Armed with three distinct bodies of recent work, Andrade first broached an exhibition of national importance in 1954, when *Souvenir*, an evocative painting of an angel fish skeleton, was included in the National Academy of Design's *129th Annual Exhibition*. When *Souvenir* was displayed a year later at the Norfolk Museum of Arts and Sciences (now the Chrysler Museum of Art), it won a purchase prize, becoming the first of her works to enter an art museum collection. In between these two events, Andrade had her first significant one-woman exhibition at the Philadelphia Art Alliance. Though she would still need commercial design commissions to pay the bills, she had clearly established the artist's career she had strived for and she would need to connect more closely with galleries, collectors, and fellow artists. In 1955, Andrade convinced her husband to return with her to Philadelphia.

In her style, media, and motivations, Andrade continued to forge ahead on multiple tracks. Public projects, such as a copper mobile, *Sea Birds*, installed in the Cheltenham Junior High School and decorative collaborations with her husband, reinforced ambitions she had long held.

> My ideal . . . was to do work with architecture, that whole idea of studying mural decoration when I was at the Academy and hoping to participate in some sort of synthesis of art and architecture.[6]

A series of watercolors and paintings produced during summer sojourns to Gloucester, Massachusetts, conversely continued the researches she had begun in her Maine drawings, now layering flat organic shapes on an underlying floral field. "I began to work more with color and I studied the writings and works of [Josef] Albers and [Paul] Klee," she explains. "I wanted to learn about painting perceptually and scientifically."[7] Incrementally, Andrade was moving toward abstraction.

A new phase in Andrade's career began in the autumn of 1957, when she taught an evening class in drawing at the Philadelphia Museum School of Art

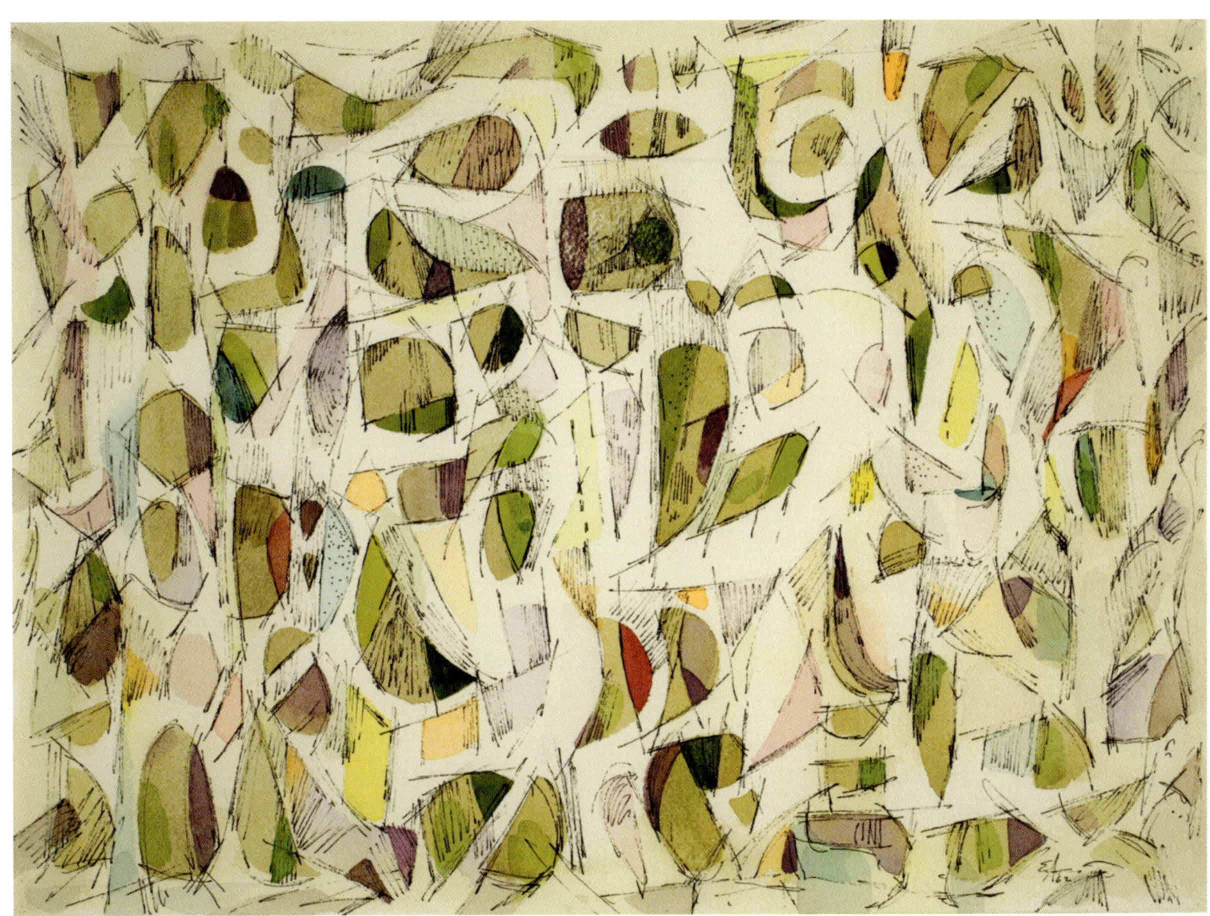

Garden Dance, 1962, cat. 11

(renamed the Philadelphia College of Art in 1964 and the University of the Arts in 1987). Promoted to a day class in Color and Design in the following year, Andrade would continue to lead the Two-Dimensional and Foundation Programs at the school for twenty-five years. The curriculum of this institution had diverged markedly from that of the Pennsylvania Academy since the early decades of the century, and Andrade's interest in Bauhaus methods and theories were encouraged, even redoubled, in her new milieu.

On her path to abstraction, Andrade had made isolated works up to this time that could properly be said to have abandoned recognizable subject matter. A solitary untitled painting produced in the mid-1950s, inspired by study of Polynesian sculpture and reminiscent of the visual vocabulary of Paul Klee, was made up of broad brown lines on a white ground, suggesting the "signs" of non-Western art without obvious reference to any corollary "signified" meaning.[8] More significantly, one of her public commissions, a mosaic mural entitled *Integration of Science and Art* that she produced in 1959–60 for the Columbia Branch (now the Cecil B. Moore Branch) of the Free Library of Philadelphia, employed a design of a large circle surrounding two smaller ones, each overlaid with a branching pattern of thick, dark lines, to produce a composition whose forms were wholly symbolic rather than imitative.[9]

It was the artist's teaching, however, that took her over the final steps to an abstract style. For her Color and Design classes, she would assign her students "problems" with colors and shapes, based upon the Bauhaus teachings of Klee, through which they might explore problems of perception: the ways colors advance and recede when placed next to others and the ease with which the eye can be manipulated and fooled by these relationships. "I became very fascinated with the problems I was giving the students," she has recounted. "I was a very conscientious teacher, so I would try them out myself."[10] Andrade's experimentation led to *Cross* (1962), a purely geometric abstraction and the first of her Op Art paintings.

In a second *Cross* painting of 1963 and in many other designs in the following years, Andrade explored a wide variety of geometric themes and variations: discrete forms and repetitious ones, rectangular shapes and round ones, verticals, horizontals, diagonals, and zigzags — a feast of visual sensations achieved by the separation of one color from another by crisply delineated edges. Her experience as an architectural draughtsman served her well in this enterprise, which relied on a uniform, precise handling of shapes and paint surfaces. Any deviation from the geometric rigor, any "personal" touch in the application of paint, would ruin the effect.

For the purposes of the present exhibition, the focus on drawings becomes at once a hurdle in these works, because few preparatory drawings to define the compositions were preserved (and without color would be only ancillary artifacts of her process, anyway), and yet also a paramount concern, because without the underlying generative diagrams the paintings would fail. These geometric paintings, in a distinctive way, transformed traditional concepts of drawing. From an artist perfectly happy to jump back and forth between media, these paintings arguably *are* drawings — ones in which penciled or inked lines have been recast as boundaries between flat planes of unmodulated pigment.

To the general public, Andrade has described her adoption of geometric abstraction in the most practical terms:

> "I was teaching a lot by then — to make a living. I had such a limited amount of time that I had to invent a way to paint that didn't just . . . depend on my mood. Something that was more like a program than a spontaneous expression of feeling." She laughs. "It's the kind of thing women have always done — like knitting! Something you can pick up when you have the time, drop when you get busy with something else, and come back exactly where you left off."
>
> She says: "The thing you learn is, you don't have to go outside yourself and paint what you experience. You learn that you can generate a painting in its own terms, by setting up a program for it. You can make the painting a metaphor for experience. Even for a quality of light. You invent a vocabulary for that."
>
> She says: "You know, I probably should've lived in Byzantine times, when there were all these rules for how you painted Jesus and how many saints had to stand on each side of him. I respond to the geometry of the composition. I like the very first moves you make, when you're deciding where to put what." She stops and thinks. "The rigging is what I like."[11]

The programmatic nature of her process, her reliance on geometry, and above all the eye-popping visual impact of many of her works contributed to Andrade's association with the Op Art movement, introduced to the public in 1965 in the Museum of Modern Art's exhibition *The Responsive Eye*, a show in which, ironically, she did not participate (the curator became aware of Andrade's paintings too late to include them). Op Art — a designation adopted in the press as an abbreviation of "optical" and a play on the contemporaneous Pop Art movement — was embraced more closely by the public and by the commercial world than it was by critics, who considered its perceptual gymnastics too decorative to be taken as seriously as the cerebral

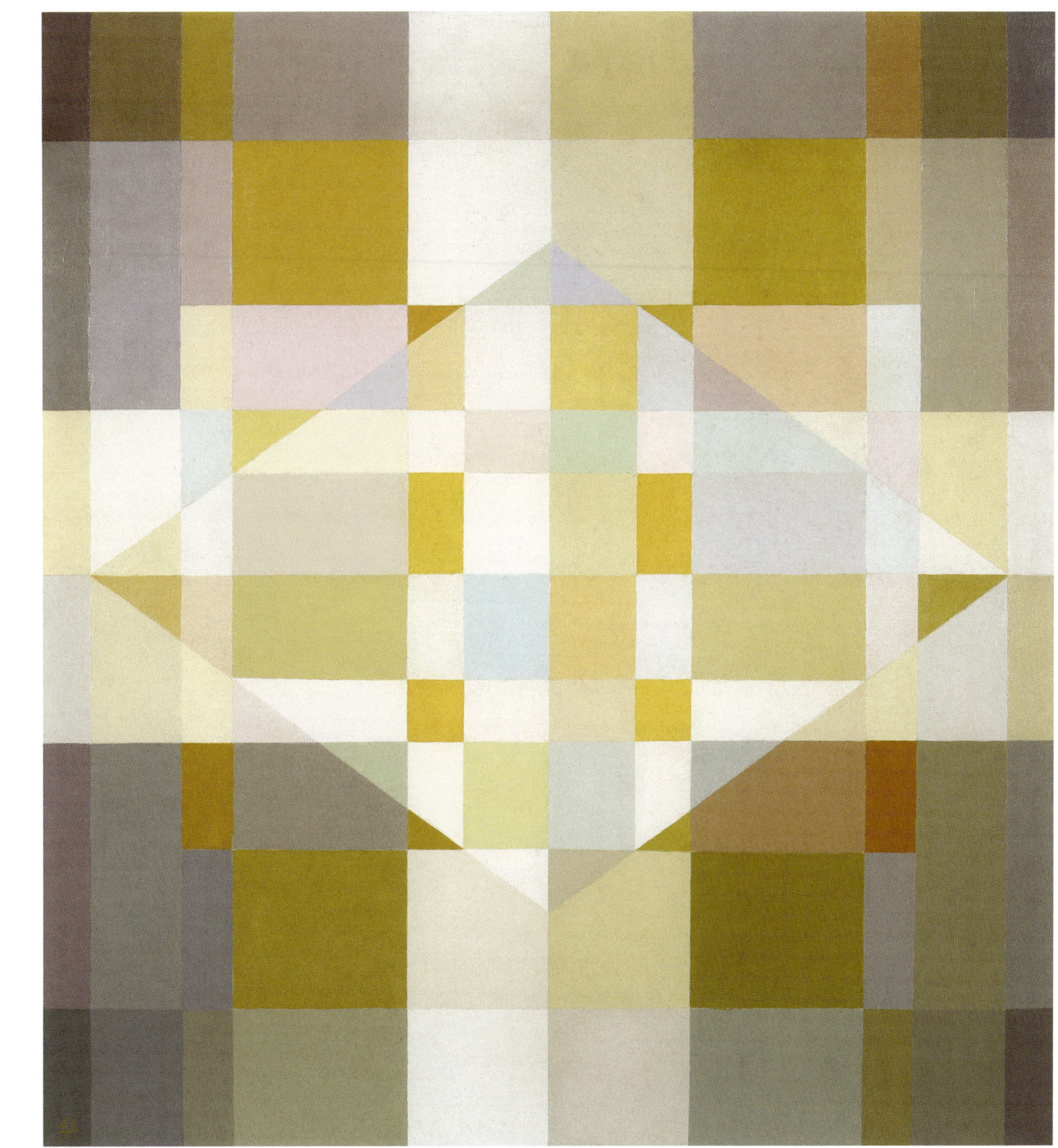

Cross, 1962, cat. 12

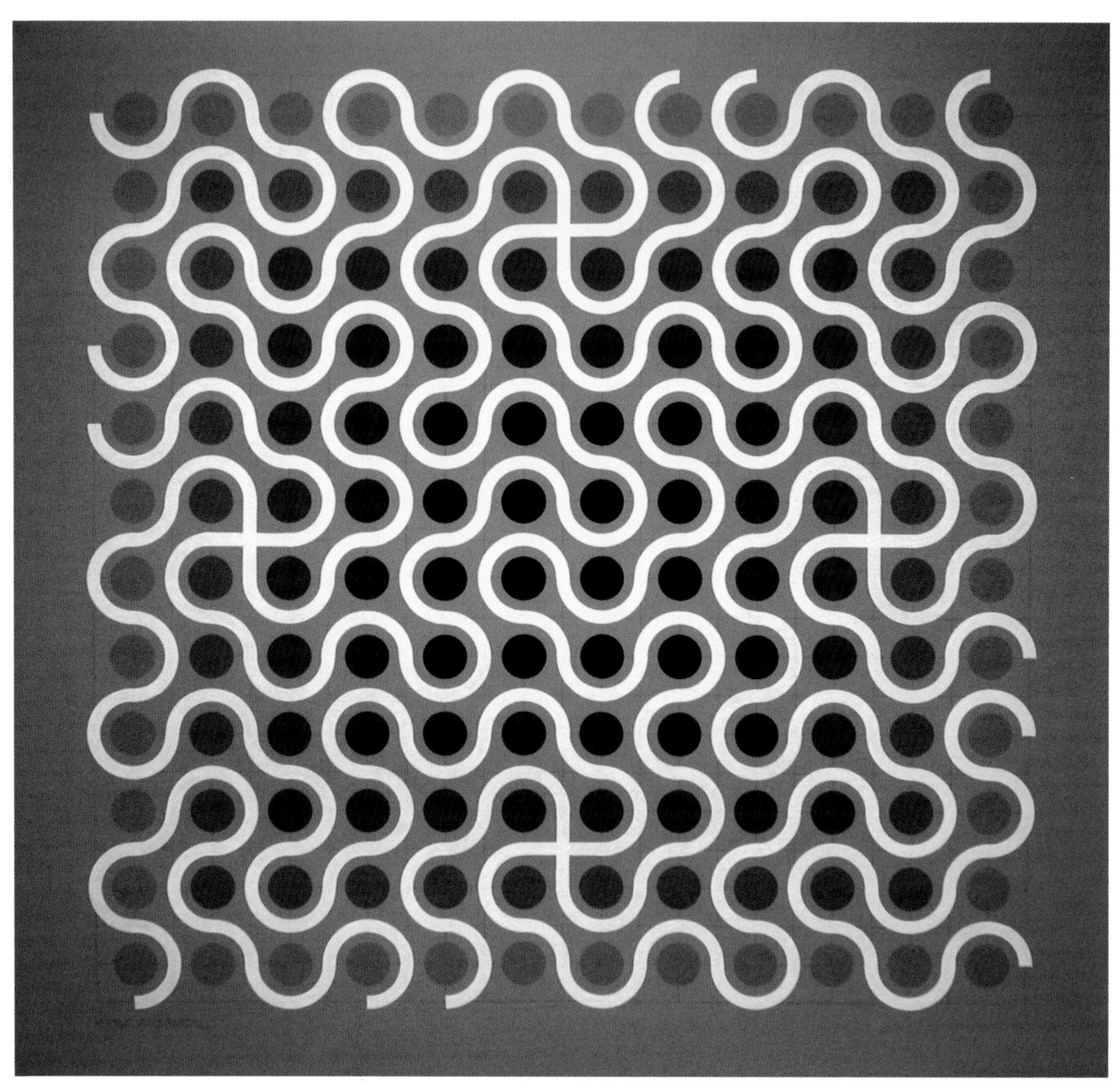

White Dragons, 1968, cat. 16

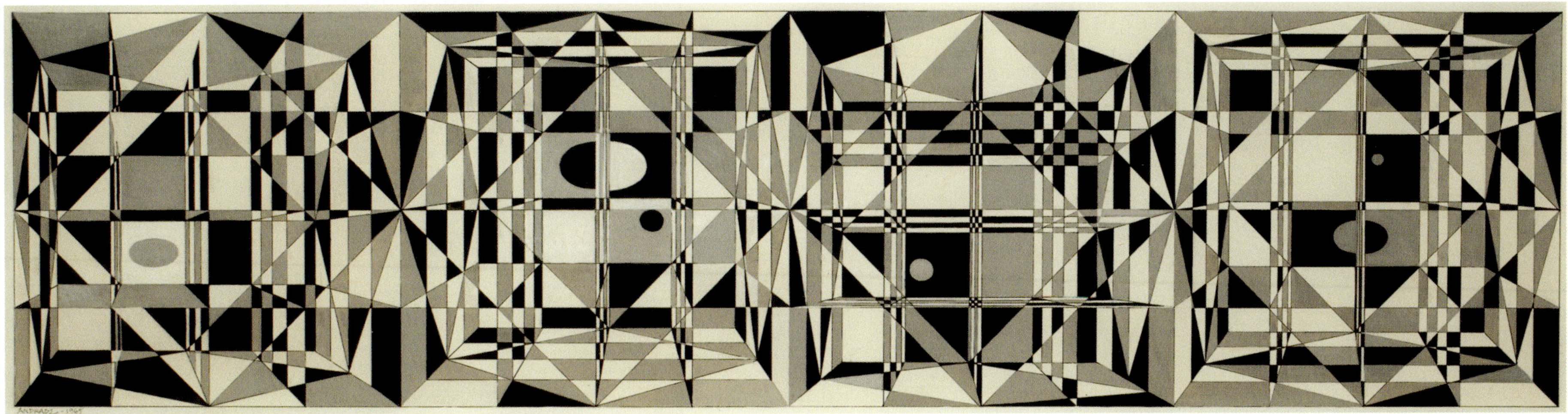

Space Frame Study, 1965, cat. 13

rhetoric and reductive sculptures and paintings of Minimalist artists of the same period. All three movements had arisen in part as a reaction to the narcissistic excesses these artists perceived in the drama-laden outpourings of Abstract Expressionist painters.[12] Andrade succinctly summed up the thoughts of many: "I think that this generation feels that you don't attempt to solve emotional and sociological problems through your art."[13]

The democratic impulse of Op painters, making works that anyone could grasp immediately, visually, viscerally, made the movement an instant darling of institutions seeking to expand their audiences, and Andrade's works were featured in a host of exhibitions throughout the country at mid-decade. The high caliber of her paintings also earned Andrade her first dealer representation at New York's East Hampton Gallery, which specialized in artists of this movement. In the intellectual circles of art commentary, however, Op Art's popular appeal and the rapid absorption of its seductive imagery in commercial products — on fabrics, on posters, or, in the case of Andrade's paintings, on jigsaw puzzles — left critics shuddering at what they perceived as a caving to the limited aspirations of the *hoi polloi.* For those defining the canon of high art, Op Art's moment in the limelight would be brief.

The dismissiveness of critics, it turns out, was misplaced. So were Andrade's own self-deprecating descriptions of her paintings as a teacher's solutions to student assignments or an alternative to knitting. Andrade's evolution to geometric abstraction had been hard-won and was rooted in a profound understanding of aesthetic and scientific theory: Michel-Eugène Chevreul on color, Hermann von Helmholtz on optics, gestalt theorists on the workings of the senses, Carl Jung on the persistence of cultural symbols, Lancelot Law Whyte on the comprehension of complex patterns.[14] Those theories, pored over for many years, lay behind every decision the artist was making. Take any one of Andrade's paintings, change any feature to the slightest degree, and the whole falls apart and loses its magic.

A decade before the feminist movement would elevate the status of crafts, few could appreciate, either, Andrade's historical couching of her intentions:

> I find myself in the ancient tradition of all those anonymous artisans who have painted pottery and tiles, laid mosaic pavings, woven baskets and carpets, embroidered vestments and sewn quilts. Our tradition reaches back through eons of time to that genius who first drew a circle and used its magic.[15]

At a time when artists desirous of success were expected to become celebrities — with Andy Warhol setting the standard — her identification with the unidentified, however skilled or innovative they might have been, in a perspective that encompassed millennia was not giving commentators

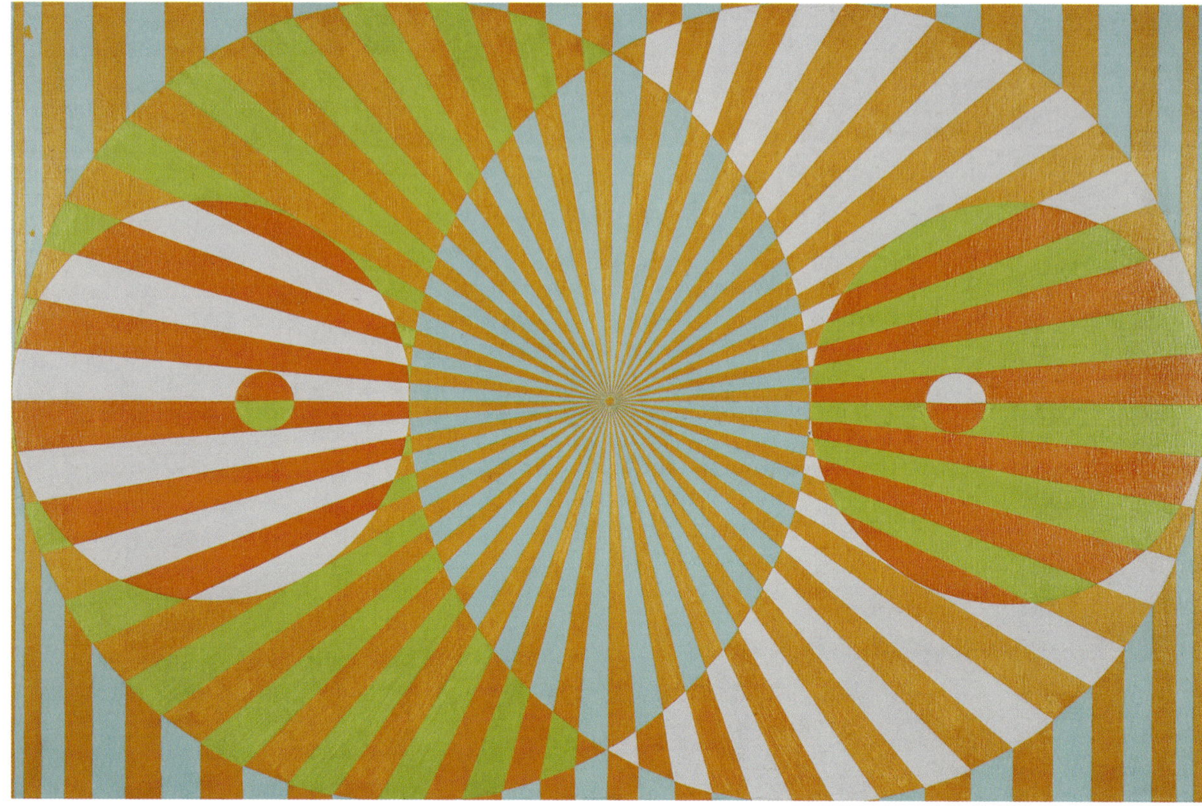

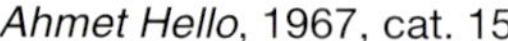
Ahmet Hello, 1967, cat. 15

the snap, crackle, and pop that sold copy and raised reputations.

Overlooked, too, were the factors that distinguished Andrade from the majority of Op artists. Her attention to an aesthetic that could be appreciated by the uninitiated was altogether appropriate for an artist steeped in the populism of the 1930s.[16] Indeed, Andrade's long-held desire to produce works wedding art and architecture might be seen to serve a parallel ambition for large, diverse, often untutored audiences that the critically acclaimed Minimalists and their advocates ignored. Four of Andrade's best-known paintings from this period she produced to reconstitute the panels she had designed for an unrealized architectural project, a four-sided *Space Frame* of incised plexiglas intended for the public lobby of a Philadelphia corporation.

Above all, it was clear from the outset that most critics missed the deeper significance of Andrade's works, that more than merely manipulating the eye of the viewer at the instant of first encounter they were meant to bring attention to the ease of creating befuddling illusions and question altogether the relationship between sensory perception and a richer, more accurate comprehension of reality. Andrade raised her concern to an artist-reporter in 1965:

> "This 'optical' label could be the kiss of death. It's too simple. It seems to refer too directly to the physiology of the eye. It fails to suggest that we are exploring the whole process of perception . . . attempting to evaluate the comparative importance of direct, visual experience, conditioning, cerebration."[17]

Another factor that would distinguish Andrade from her Op Art peers would become more evident in her works of the 1970s.

Andrade had been steadily expanding her vocabulary of geometry, and her media for exploiting it, for a decade when she received a commission to design stone paving for Philadelphia's Salvation Army Headquarters. For the floor of a semi-enclosed court she conceived a scheme of overlapping circles, laid out in concentric arcs of cobblestones, intersecting other such arcs, like the oversized tesserae of an ancient mosaic. The patterns she developed in preparation for this project led, in turn, to one of her most famous series of paintings, begun in 1973. In each of these paintings, through many variations, radiating sets of lines abut or oppose other radial patterns, each line sparely drawn with a ruling pen, most often in a delicate pale hue upon a uniform background of a single dark color. Gone were the jarring, brash color contrasts and broad planes of her paintings of the 1960s. In their place, the motion, the illusion, and the drama of each work relied on subtler color combinations and the gentler but no less insistent directionality of close, converging or diverging lines.

Overnight, it seems, when these paintings were first exhibited *en masse*, commentary on Andrade's paintings took a decided turn. Everyone reported that the forms had their derivation in geometry, most obvious in the independent drawings the artist made in the series, drawn in graphite on white paper with only a thin line of ruled color as a "spine" from which the graphite lines radiated. This new geometry, so different from her 1960s works, was characterized as "contemplative . . . suffused with poetry," "idyllic," "serene, yet energized," "they mesmerize."[18] But also as one, curators and critics described the effects of the new paintings through analogies to the natural world: light glinting off spider webs, the translucent rays of a fish skeleton, the hypnotic movement of ocean waves, atmospheric and celestial effects. One reviewer, citing the artist's own words, made oblique reference to those most Romantic of concepts: Transcendentalism and the Sublime.[19] A consensus emerged that there was *content.* And that raised speculation of whether there might always have been content underlying Andrade's abstractions, and just what that content was.

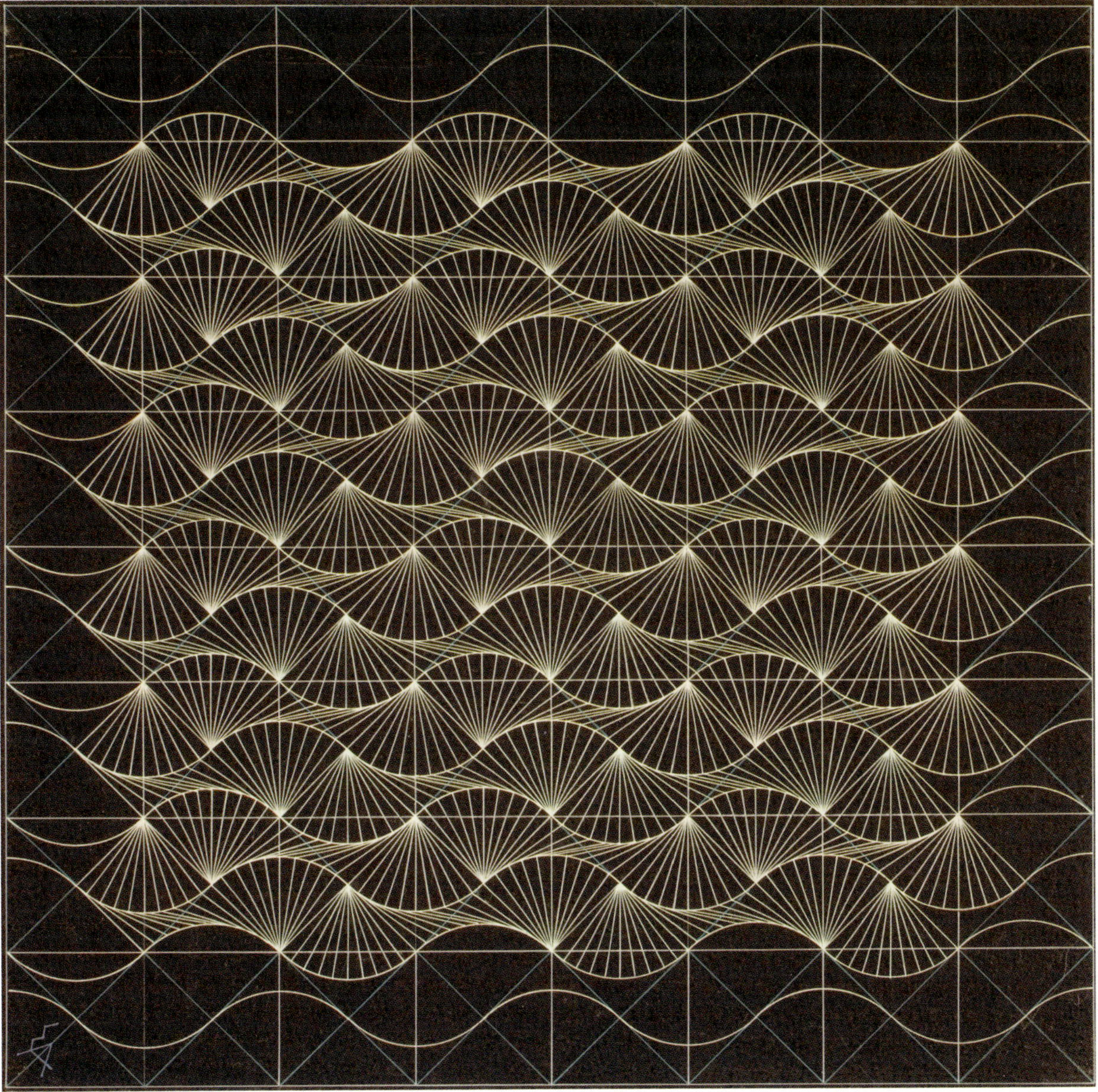

Gray Lake, 1976, cat. 25

The artist effectively confirmed (or inspired?) these natural associations with the titles she chose for paintings in this new series. Her 1960s abstractions most often had borne neutral titles, such as

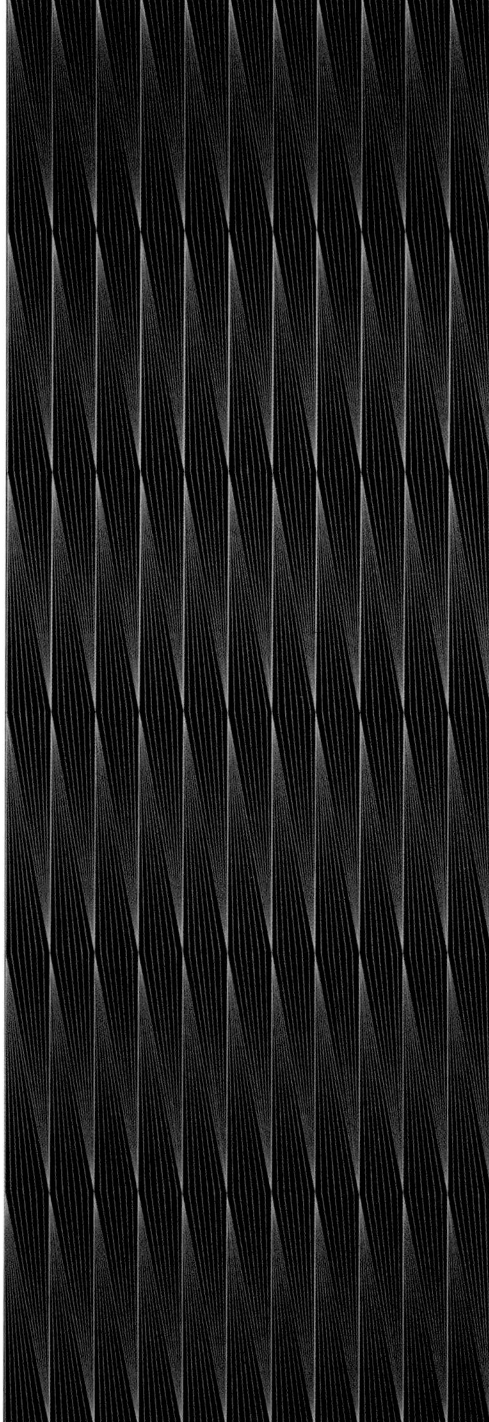

Geometric 4–63 (1963), *Color Motion 2–64* (1964), *Falling Cubes* (1966), or the mandala-like *Criss-Cross* (1970); occasionally, space-age metaphors would arise, as in *Cold Planet, Hot Planet* (both 1965), and *Space Dream* (1970). Some titles in the new series extended the references to encompass generic physical forces: *Torsion* (1973), *Ignition* (1975), and *Acceleration* (1977). But the majority of these paintings after 1973 bore titles that unabashedly alluded to natural phenomena we could almost reach out and touch: *Spring Veils* (1973), *Cool Wave* (1974), *Gray Lake* (1976), *Ebbtide* (1976), *Updraught* (1976), and *Night Sea* (1977).

Andrade, when asked outright about content in her abstract works, even by her admirers, has been reticent to hand out the tools for her own dissection.

From 2003, in reference to her geometric paintings: "Form and color — what you see is what you get. There's no story that comes with that."[20]

From a 1997 interview: "I am far more concerned with the purely visual than with the narrative, expressionistic or romantic aspects of painting. I am interested in formal structure both in the natural realm and in art."[21]

Returning to 2003: "If you bring anything to it, it may have some symbolic value for you, and it may have some symbolic value for me. But that's after I've done it."[22]

Tensor, 1975, cat. 22

And yet, from 1965, at the outset of her geometric work: "I find myself in the ancient tradition of all those anonymous artisans. Artists have always used the pure and powerful archetypes, the circle, the triangle, the square, the pentagon, and endowed them with symbolic content."[23]

And in 1971: "Geometry is a tool for describing the natural world, a way to diagram its richly varied structures of relations. The geometric arrangements observed in both organic and inorganic systems have found expression in the arts of every period in history. My own painting is made in celebration of form and order and seeks to continue the long tradition of geometry as metaphor."[24]

To dwell on this issue of content today, when we have become accustomed to a pluralist and permissive contemporary art scene, may seem vaguely quaint, but in the early 1970s artists and critics were only beginning to unlock themselves from the entrenched polemics with which abstractionists had won high stature in the art world of the 1960s. With the demise of Abstract Expressionism's emotional outpourings of self, the succeeding generation — Color Field painters, Minimalists, etc. — extolled the primacy of paintings and sculptures about painting and sculpture: about the picture plane or mass, about the boundaries of the objects, about their materials. As these artists gained critical acclaim for

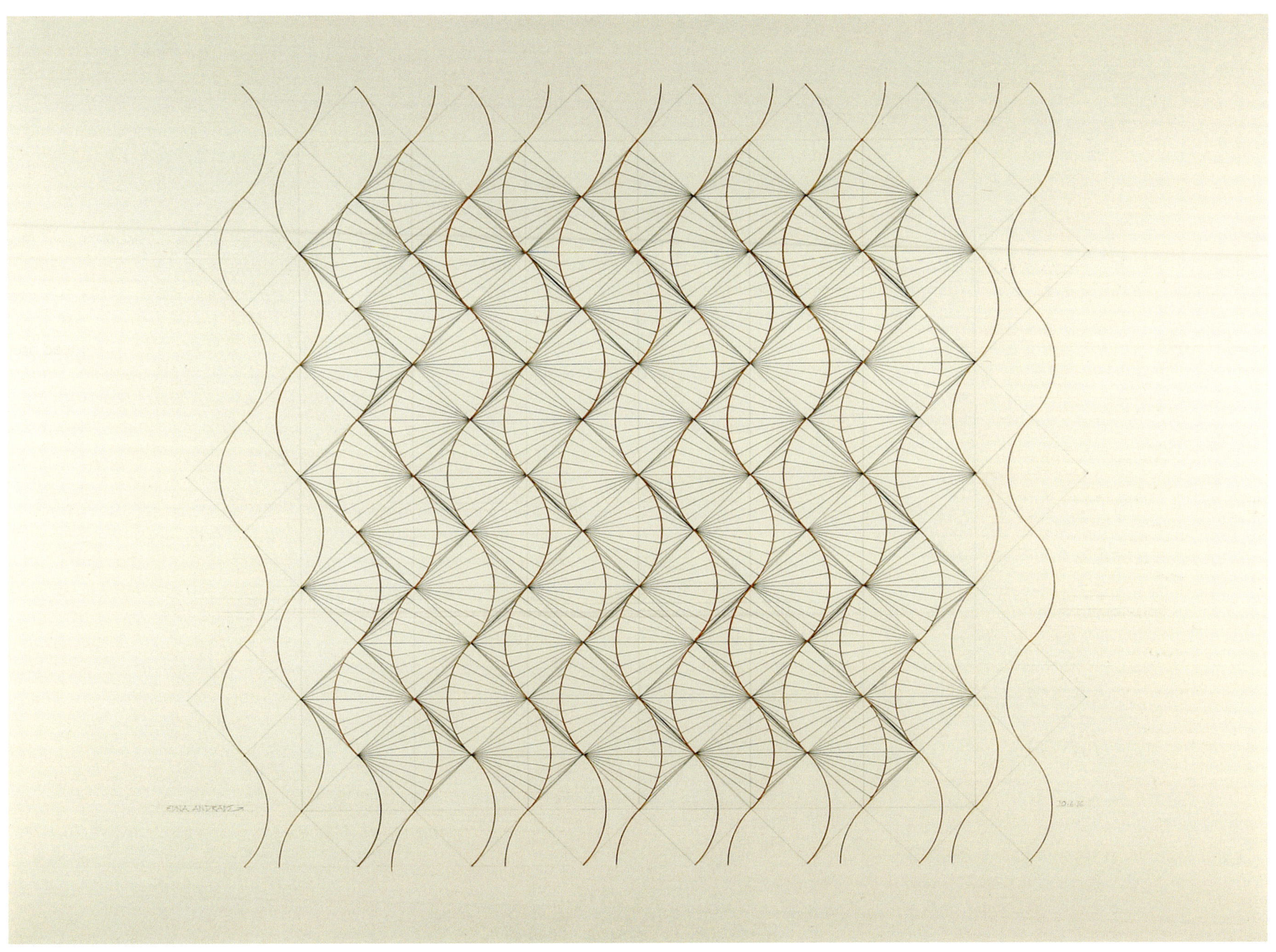

Drawing 10/6/76, 1976, cat. 23

stripping their artworks of the messiness of external associations, they turned their backs on the aesthetic ramifications of turn-of-the-century Symbolist or Theosophical theory — the conviction that if naturalistic painting was best suited to the nineteenth century's empiricism, so abstract forms and compositions were best suited to communicating universal, transient, or ethereal ideas or states of mind that were essential to a new age — that had led the first-generation abstractionists to break with tradition in the first place.

Andrade's paintings challenged the new regime. Her works might share some of the attributes championed by the dominant formalist camp: they were often composed as fields, without a hierarchic concentration of pictorial emphasis in any one area; they generally respected the borders of the composition; and surely the 1970s works, composed only of lines of color, took the fusion of drawing and painting to a level seldom seen since Jackson Pollock's drip paintings. But they also did the unthinkable: they admitted metaphor. They referenced nature not with a mimesis of its surface manifestations but with equivalents of the enduring order beneath. Andrade was restoring a subject, albeit a perhaps ineffable one, to abstract art. And that subject inarguably moved the viewers of her works.

By the late 1970s, the art world was becoming less monolithic, less exclusionary, and the nation's museums, galleries, and art magazines began to acknowledge and trumpet the works of artists working in a wide variety of styles that had been developing for some time under the public's radar. Landscape, still-life, and figure painting were treated to a comeback with the popularity of Photo-Realism, and even the most dedicated abstractionists found the world would not come crashing down if they dared to essay representation. Andrade took this opportunity — briefly — to experiment with traditional modes of illusion in *trompe-l'oeil* drawings that gave three-dimensionality to the elemental forms she had extolled in the 1960s. Cones, cylinders, cubes, and pyramids of a uniform whiteness, awash in a no less insistently white light, were represented in soft gradations of colored pencil as if they were an exercise in modeling. The artist was momentarily re-examining her vocabulary, but the resulting imagery and discipline would be banked for future use.

Intriguingly, one of the favorite analogies of Symbolist artists and the first-generation abstractionists, and even of James A. McNeill Whistler before them, proposed parallel means and aims between non-representational art (or art that at least took considerable liberties with appearances) and music, which relied foremost for its expression on a non-descriptive structure of sequential tones and cadence. In what is almost certainly a coincidence, it was precisely toward equivalences in this direction that Andrade moved next, with acrylic studies and paintings appropriately titled *Fanfare* and *Crescendo*. She described the paintings in a letter:

> In the transitional paintings shown here, I began to experiment with illusions of luminosity which gradations of color may generate. In order to concentrate more fully on the scales of chromatic color and to diminish the allure of pattern, I used a very simple stripe and grid structures to contain the color activity.
>
> As several of the titles of these paintings suggest, I thought about my arrays of color in terms of music. I tried to make certain juxtapositions of color "notes" evoke qualities of musical tones.[25]

Fanfare and *Crescendo*, while clearly a momentary stage in the artist's expansion of her painterly means and preoccupations, signaled a return more generally to brighter color in Andrade's works, after a decade's absence. A semester in Arizona in 1981 gave new priority to this heightened palette and to a simpler geometry as Andrade became captivated by the forms, colors, and light of the desert, the mountains, the cacti, and Western skies. In Arizona and on her return to Philadelphia, she also reprised a medium, collage, that she had employed only briefly in the early 1960s during her transition into abstraction.

For the series of collages and paintings she would make over three years recapturing her experience of the West, Andrade took as her compositional building blocks the sparest of shapes — the square, the triangle, and the circle, painted in a rich range of graduated, mixed colors — which she repeated and stacked and overlapped in arrangements that at times were symphonic in their variety and at other times approached the joyous topographic shorthand of folk art. Drawings she made at this time in colored pencil gave her a chance to test compositions and color combinations for the paintings, but they also offered textural effects that allowed her to weave her shapes as if they were transparent. In their complexity and gracious tactility these drawings often exceed the resultant paintings for their emotive appeal.

Another trip in 1984, this time to India, was equally generous in the formal vocabulary and vibrant colors it offered to Andrade, who returned to make elaborate drawings in colored pencil or ruled acrylic pigment re-envisioning the maze-like grid of Islamic tile patterns. Her visit on this trip to the eighteenth-century architectural observatory of Jaipur gave her an oversized still life of extruded shapes, which she

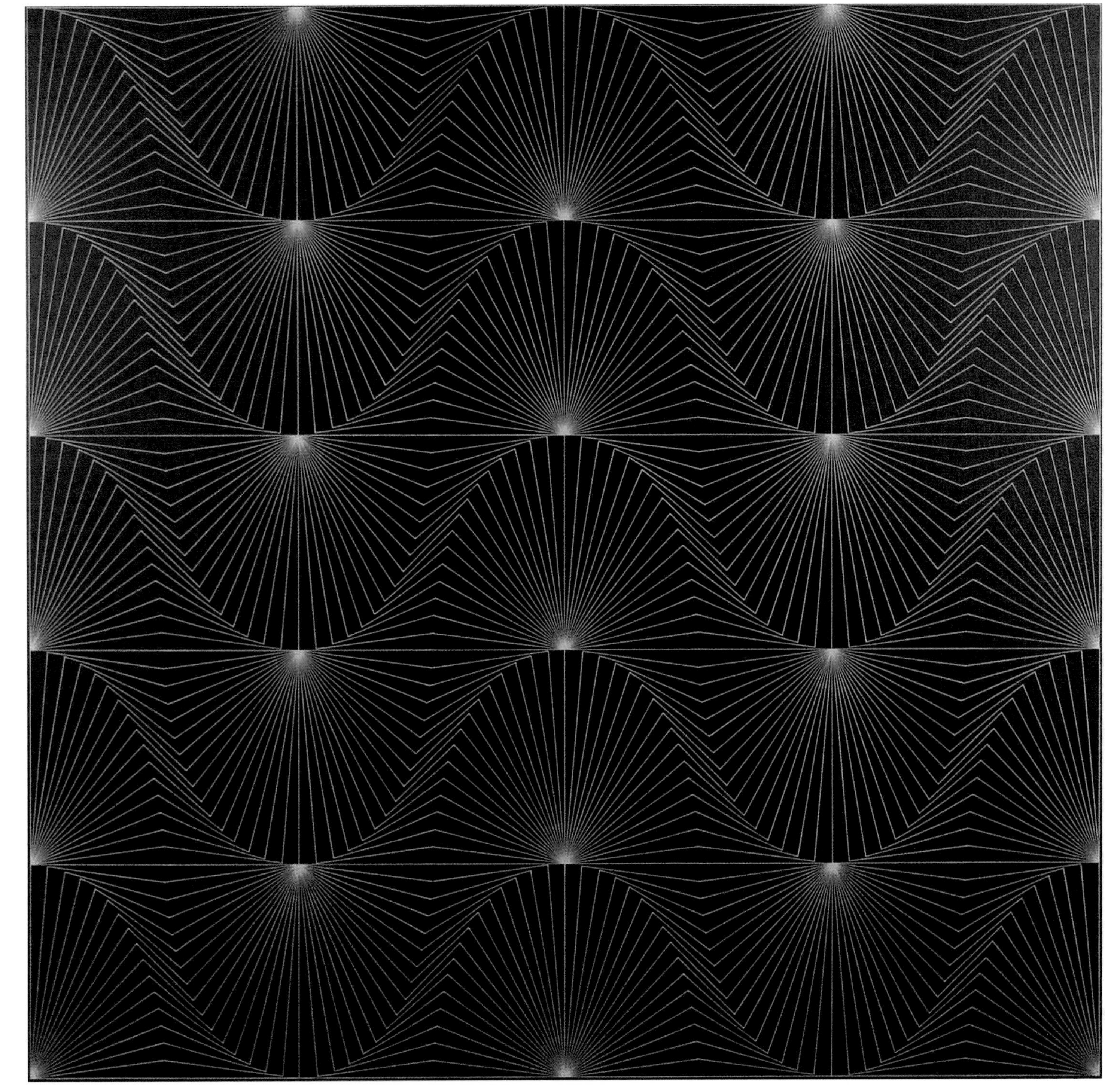

Untitled, 1980, cat. 31

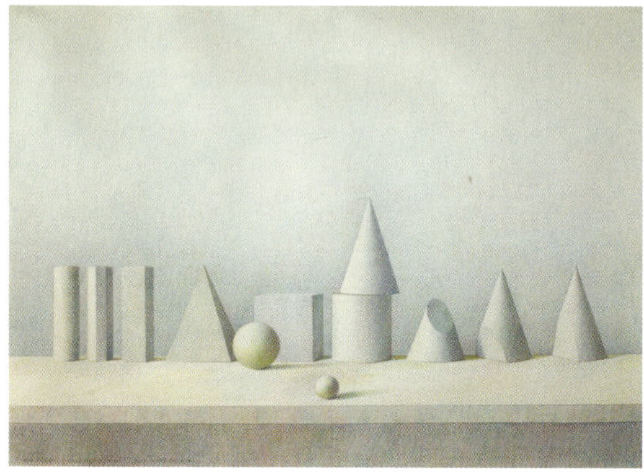

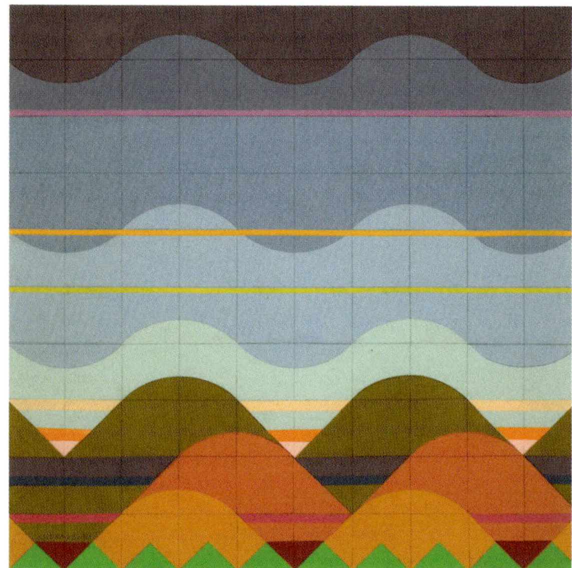

Top: *Cones, Pyramids, and Prisms*, 1978, cat. 27
Below: *Painted Desert Blue*, 1983, cat. 33

reconfigured, bathed in a *trompe-l'oeil*-style raking light, and rearranged in rows, piles, and floating sprays across her compositions.

Each of these series brought into high relief the tumbling inventiveness that distinguishes Andrade's career, her propensity not only to investigate media and pictorial solutions that are new to her but also to return to ones she once took up and set aside years or even decades earlier. For all of the apparent changes of their outward style, her works ultimately have answered to the same fundamental preoccupations: the structure of the natural world, the ways we perceive that order, and the symbolic vocabulary we share to represent it. It then is perhaps not so surprising to hear that "Andrade has always maintained that she is a landscape painter, however abstract her imagery may be."[26] Andrade began her studies at the Pennsylvania Academy as a landscape painter, she re-entered the art world after World War II with drawings of the Maine coastline, she extolled symbolic content in her geometric abstractions with paintings that bore titles of landscape subjects, and she predicated her two series of early 1980s imagery on encounters with landscapes and qualities of light that captivated her. Andrade would reinvent her art twice more with landscape subjects of the New England coastline that had given her her start.

In the mid-1980s Andrade resumed her summer sojourns in Maine, this time on Great Cranberry Island. The Atlantic coast in this area is a battered one, but one, too, that is composed of the most enduring of granites. The forms of that coastline reveal themselves and the forces of their creation at the grandest and most minute scales. Both would give Andrade the substance for new bodies of work.

The first series overlapped chronologically, and sometimes pictorially, her continuing investigations of architectural imagery based on the Jaipur observatory. Collage became the hallmark of this new series: cut and torn paper layered with acrylic paint, watercolor, graphite, and wax rubbings of driftwood she would find on the beach that seemed to let the results of natural processes speak on their own behalf. These layers, standing in for the stone beach, water, hill, and more hills farther in the distance, were stacked in horizontal bands rising up the surface of the composition, much as the pyramids and circles in the artist's more ideographic Arizona landscape collages had been. Occasionally, like a visitor from India or from her *trompe-l'oeil* still lifes of the 1970s, incongruent geometric solids or illusionistic images of polished beach stones would be added in the foreground, over the overlapping layers of collage. Maybe flat circles and ellipses would disport themselves as moon and planets in the sky or more cryptically across the entire image, much as an oversized shell had mysteriously hovered in the sky above a bather in one of her 1950s paintings.

Though the subject matter was never in doubt, the emphasis in these collages was on the proportions and values of the bands and on texture, most notable in the wood grain of the rubbings that could substitute for waves on the sea or clouds in the sky — all obeisant to the same fundamental order — and in the broad dark line of the crests of hills, created where the torn paper absorbed more pigment. And though the technique might remind viewers of the late cutouts of Henri Matisse, above all in the sheer confidence of their mastery, we are never in doubt that these are the work of a quite different sensibility, one no less joyful but also one that feels equally

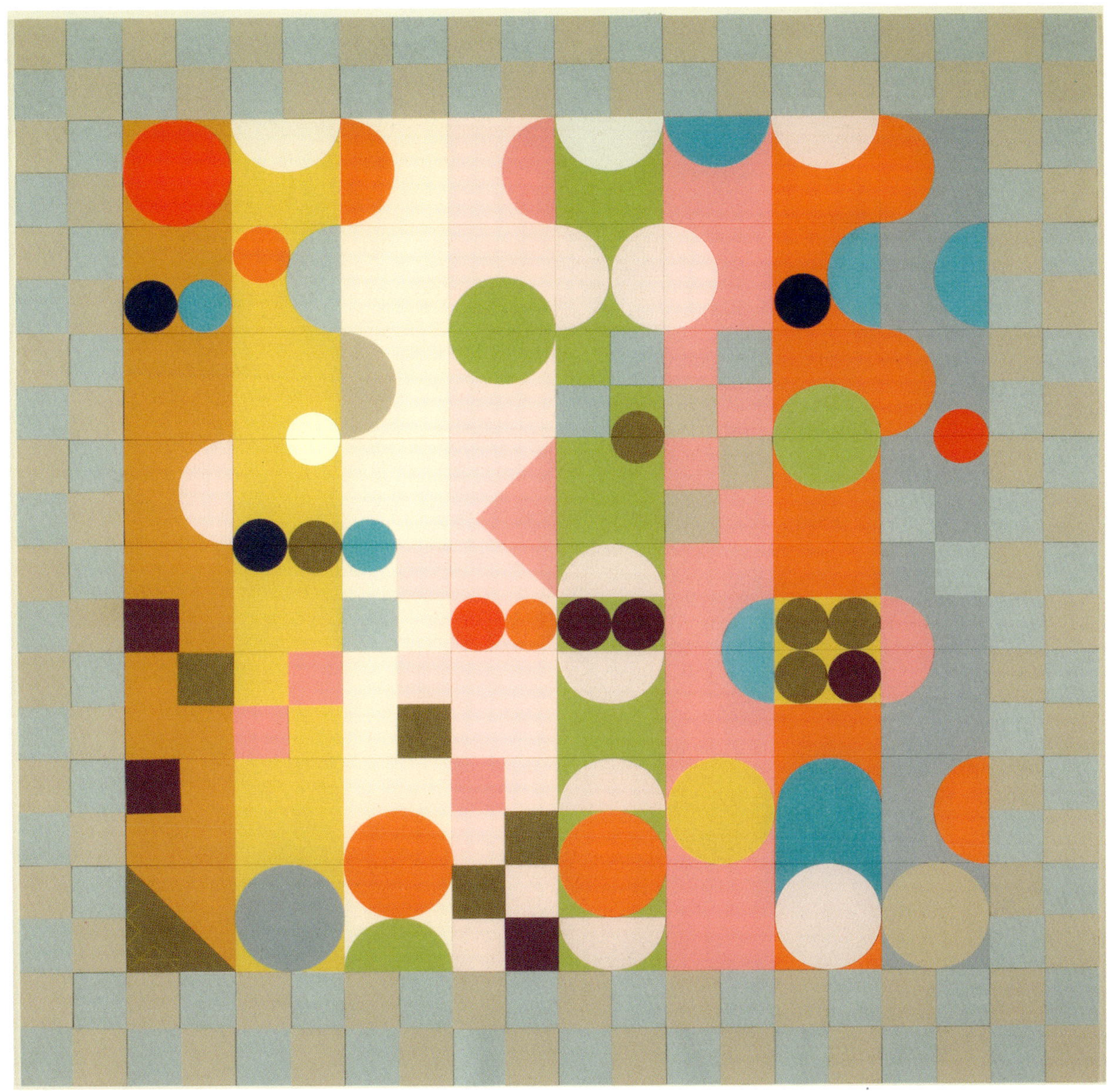

Arizona Celebration, 1981, cat. 32

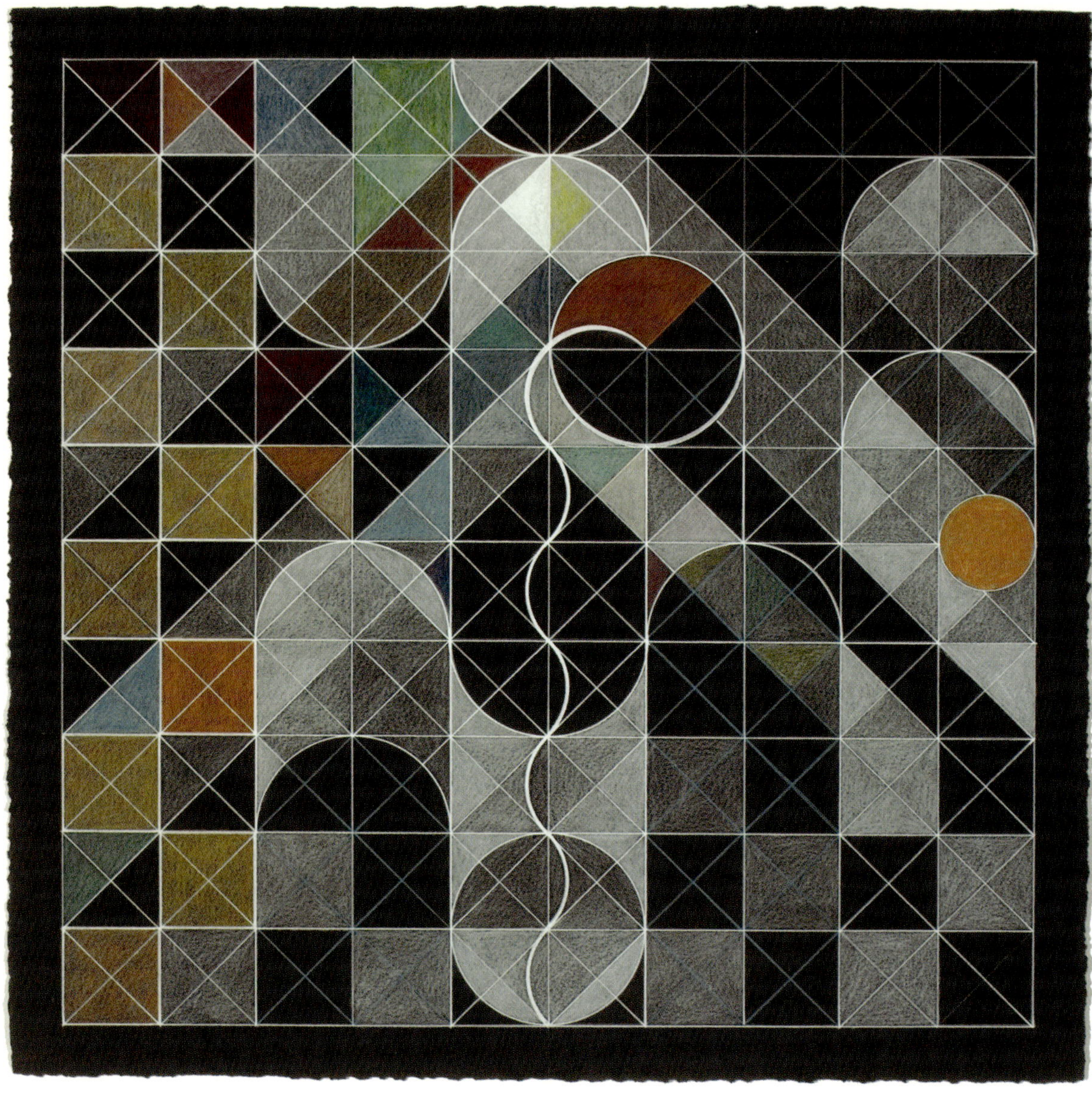

Moon Rise I, 1983, cat. 34

at home digging at the subterranean roots of everyday appearances.

From the early 1990s and extending to the present day has come the most recent series in Andrade's *oeuvre*. At last, in these works, the artist has returned not only to her earliest subject but also to her earliest medium, a most traditional medium of drawing, the graphite pencil. At this time, too, Andrade has reprised the traditional language of representation, with meticulous renderings of the contours, cracks, and fissures of the great stones that punctuate the island's edge.

The paintings that Andrade has made in this series, in delicate, near-pastel hues, are bold yet gracious investigations of the massing more than the surface of these stones. It is the drawings, though, that are the *tours de force*. Often larger in size, sometimes drawn on canvas as if usurping the exalted status of painting, these drawings are studies of monumentality and detail, two distinct and often-antithetical goals achieved here simultaneously, seamlessly. The emphasis in the drawings is on the rocks' surfaces, natural grids of eroded, rippled crystalline structure, rendered in the most unflinching and crispest of lights. The most companionable of these drawings offer glimpses to the sea and neighboring islands, rendered as flat bands of watercolor or acrylic pigment. More abstract are those that admit only a small slice of pale sky — gray, alabaster, or the subtlest of pinks — absent any gradation of atmospheric perspective. The most relentless of these works, however, exclude any sense of external boundedness, any reference to a differently textured or complexioned world beyond what is presented to us within these close-cropped frames, as they compulsively, hypnotically home in on their subject with a brutal poetry.

Drawing is seldom the facet of a career through which historians will try to trace the evolution of an artist. More often, exhibitions of drawings are a diverting side excursion to a grand tour mapped in paintings or sculpture. In the current exhibition and in this discussion, moreover, we have chosen to define drawing rather loosely, to include media and methods of notation not customarily thought of in such terms, in large part because the artist has done the same herself, over and over again. In the case of Edna Andrade, unusually, distinctively, drawing is the path that visits all of the regions she has explored. In her most recent series of drawings of the Maine coastline, Andrade, in a sense, has come home from her peregrinations. She set out to fathom "the rigging" of nature through direct observation and study, then took it apart and challenged us to acknowledge how little we understood it, then restored it to its accustomed synthesis, then manipulated it, turning it back and forth in her deft hands, and finally, when she sensed that she — and we — might really grasp it, she brought us back, enthralled, to direct observation and study of its wonders.

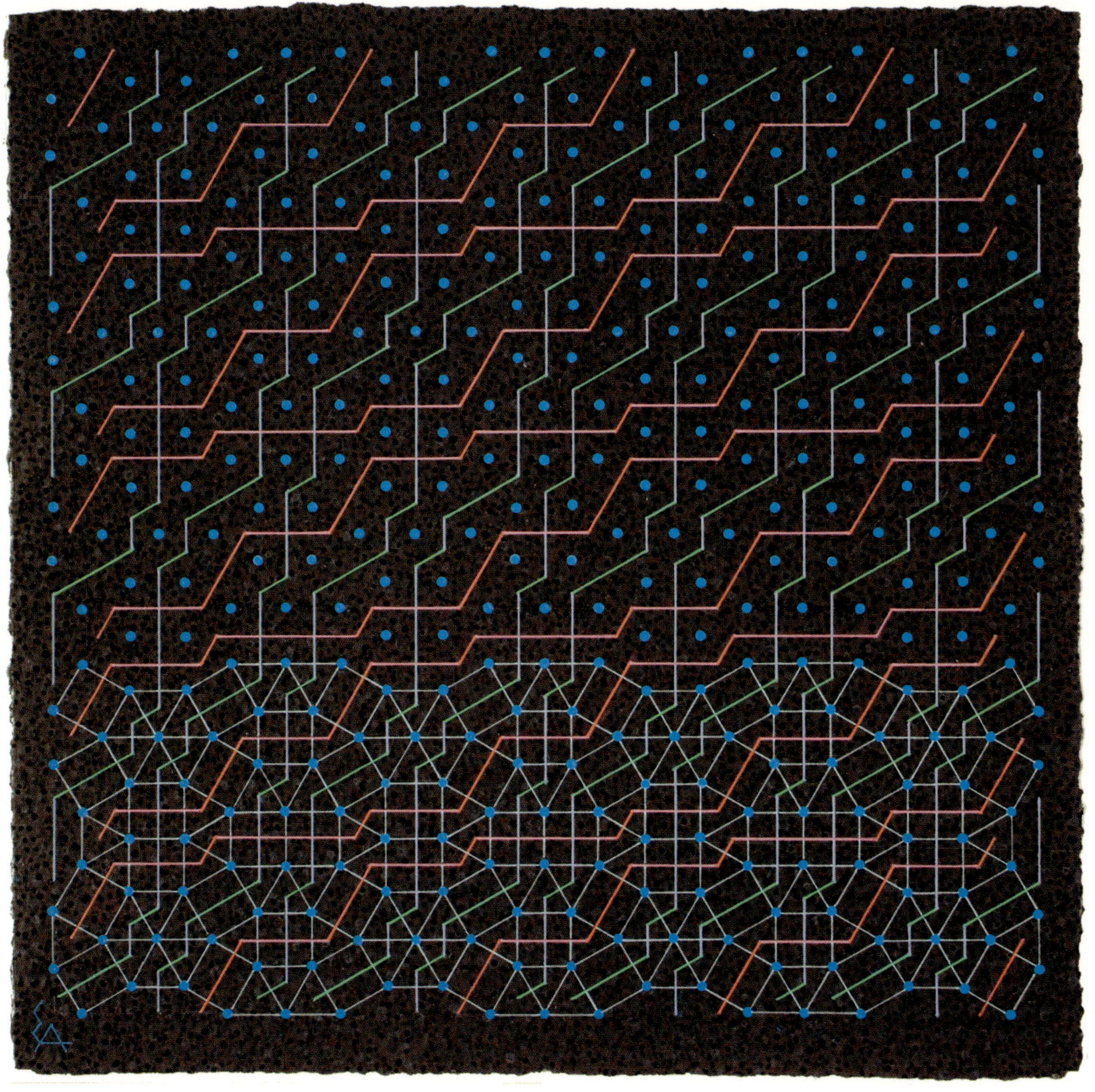

Indian Storm, 1984, cat. 37

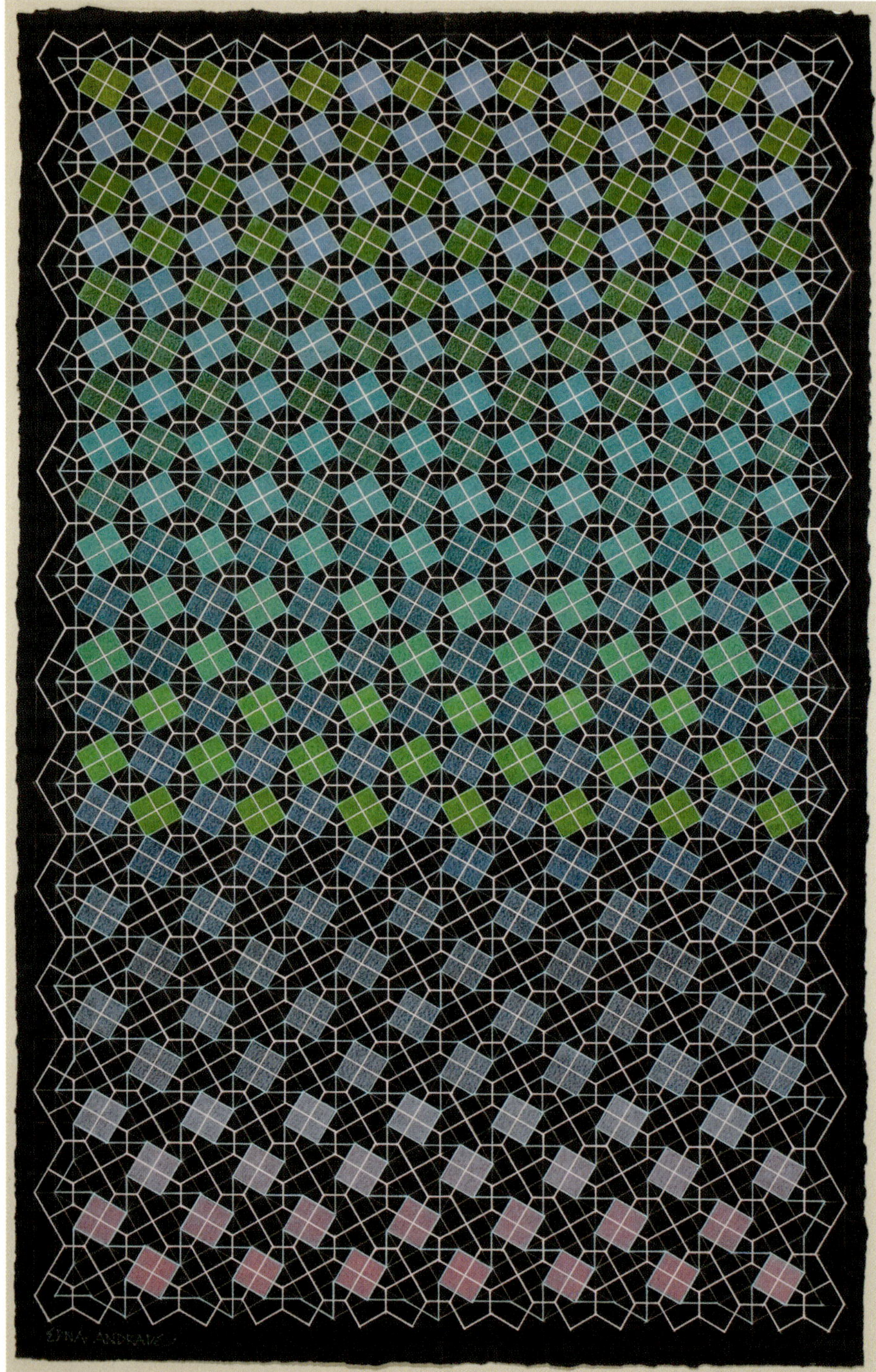

Arabian Sea, 1984, cat. 38

Some years ago, Andrade was enticed by an interviewer to recount her artistic journey. Amid the vivid anecdotes and distillations of a long and prestigious career, the conversation turned to the first steps she took on that path as a young girl in Virginia:

> "You couldn't have a childhood like I had, today. My father ran a sawmill. We lived on the edge of the swamp. There wasn't a neighbor you could see. The kids we played with were black, mostly. Of course, you were supposed to cut that out when you reached puberty. And I knew witches! Aunt Sarah, an old black woman. She was a fisherwoman, too. You'd see her walking along the road, down to the creek. You weren't supposed to talk to her. She was a conjurer. 'Watch out for that conja' woman,' the black people would say. But I knew a shortcut to the creek, so I'd run around and come up beside her. She'd make you sit down and be quiet and still. *Ssshhh*, is all she'd say, and put a finger to your lips. Then she'd show you all the things around you you never saw for yourself. Little bugs on the water. Birds in trees. Snakes. Animals. All you had to do was sit and watch where she pointed, never saying a word. 'Watch out, she'll conja' you,' the black ladies would say. I never paid any mind. But," Edna Andrade smiles, "that's what she did. Conja'd me, till I could see."[27]

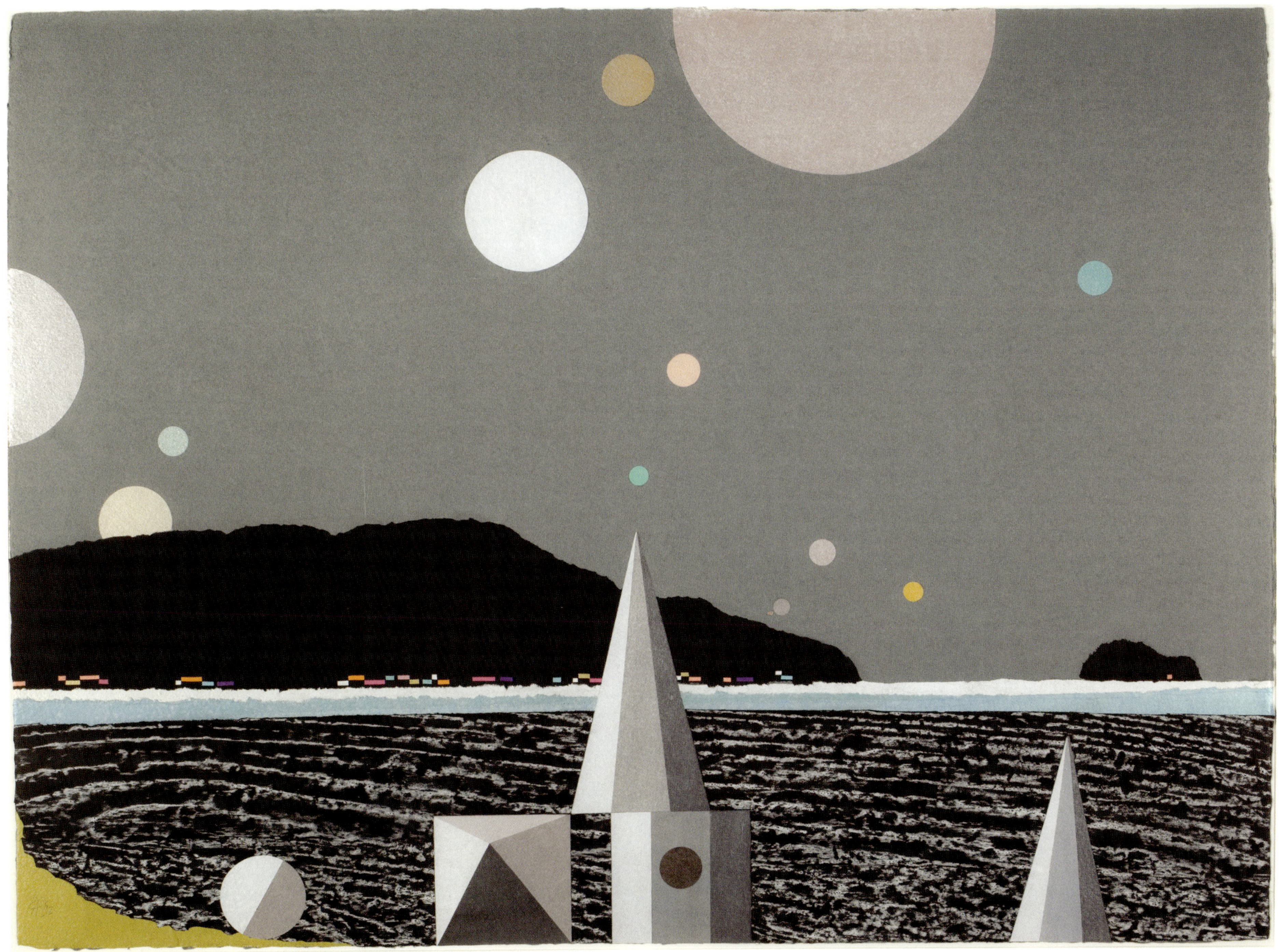

Moonlight, 1992, cat. 45

Notes to the text

1. This essay's title comes from Andrade's comments quoted in Katherine Stiles Cogan, "Alumni Profile: Edna Andrade, Painter, Printmaker, Professor Emeritus and 'Romantic Geometer,'" *Perspective*, vol. 2, no. 1 (1986), p. 6.

2. Pennsylvania Academy of the Fine Arts, *Cool Waves and Hot Blocks: The Art of Edna Andrade*, September 18, 1993–January 31, 1994, with an essay by Ann Sutherland Harris; and Institute of Contemporary Art, *Edna Andrade: Optical Paintings, 1963–1986*, January 18–April 6, 2003, with essays by Debra Bricker Balken and Ingrid Schaffner. Bravely taking up the challenge of characterizing Andrade's significance, the authors of all three essays have produced the most extensive and perceptive accounts of this artist and her works.

3. In conversations with the author (October 2006), Andrade has stated that during her studies at the Pennsylvania Academy of the Fine Arts she had only a vague awareness that Alexey Brodovitch was introducing Bauhaus-inspired experiments to his students only a few blocks away at the Pennsylvania Museum School of Industrial Art. Art education in most American schools in the 1930s was based on the methods of the Ecole des Beaux-Arts in Paris, where students first drew from plaster casts before being admitted to classes where they could draw, paint, or sculpt from nude models. The emphasis was on figure subjects, just as the themes of fine art thought most worthy by the creators of this curriculum were biblical and historical scenes. The Bauhaus revolutionized art teaching by removing recognizable subject and representation altogether to concentrate on the means to make any image: the drawn line, color, shape (usually geometric in Bauhaus practice), perception, and materials. In Germany, too, the Bauhaus stressed a political dimension to art-making that would result in a classless society of artisans, designing not only art but also utilitarian objects and the spaces in which they would be used. When the new teaching method was introduced in America after the mid-1930s, the utopian politics was most often subordinated. Today, almost all art instruction in the United States is based on the Bauhaus method; the Pennsylvania Academy remains a rare exception — and the most prestigious one — maintaining the Beaux-Arts curriculum.

4. Cogan, "Alumni Profile," p. 6.

5. Cogan, "Alumni Profile," p. 6.

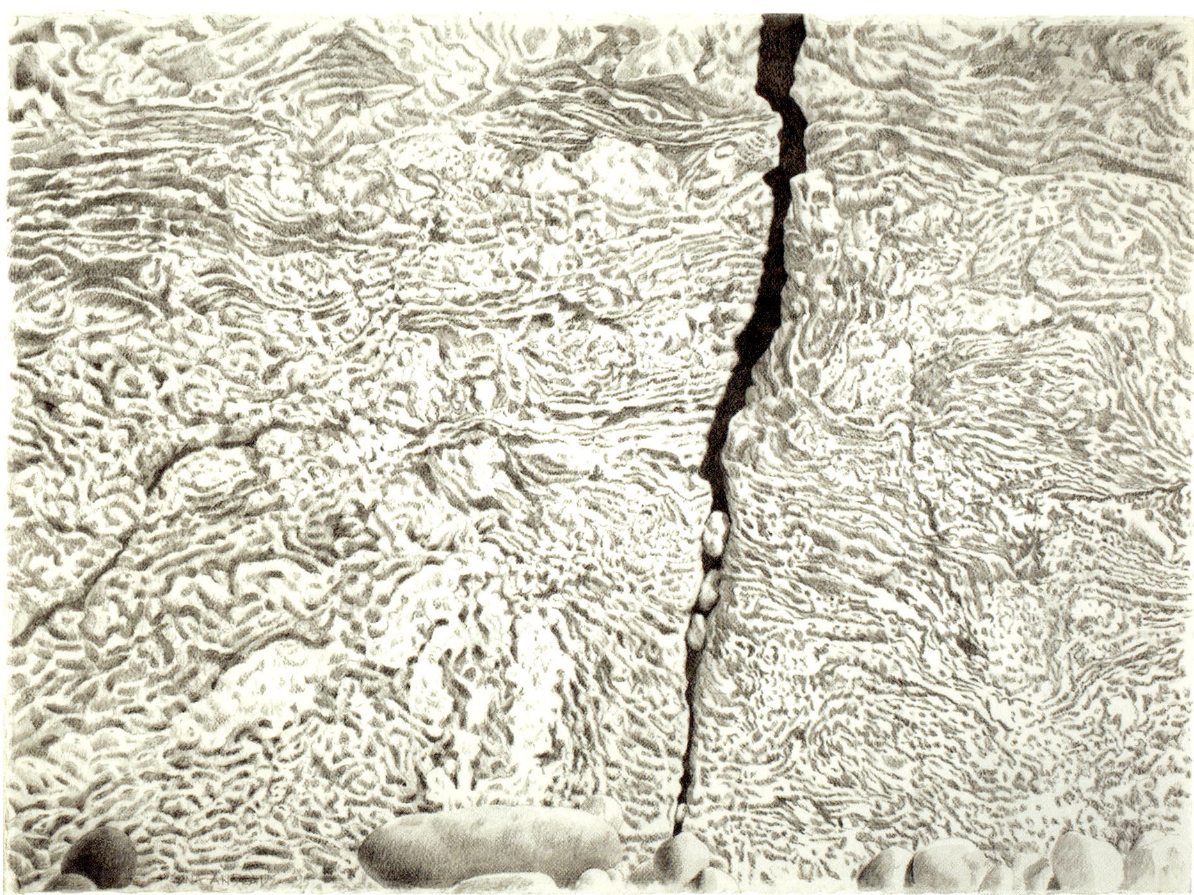

Crevice, 1995, cat. 47

6. Edna Andrade, interview by Patricia Likos, Philadelphia, April 29, 1987, typescript, p. 1, Archives of American Art/Smithsonian Institution, Washington, D.C.

7. Cogan, "Alumni Profile," p. 6.

8. This painting (in the collection of the artist), incorrectly dated 1949 on the reverse, was made, she has said, after a 1956 commission for reproductions of Polynesian sculptures for the Matson Line. Edna Andrade, interview with the author, Philadelphia, October 2006. It is possible, of course, that this work's signs do have a meaning that the artist is not disclosing.

9. Edna Andrade, "Artist's Statement on Making the Mosaic Mural at the Cecil B. Moore Branch of the Free Library of Philadelphia," April 18, 2000, collection of the artist.

10. Edna Andrade, interview by Patricia Likos, Philadelphia, April 12, 1987, typescript, p. 20, Archives of American Art/Smithsonian Institution, Washington, D.C.

11. Jim Quinn, "Driven to Abstraction," *The Philadelphia Inquirer Magazine*, April 2, 1989, p. 42.

12. Op Art's position in the context of other contemporary art movements is more extensively discussed in Debra Bricker Balken, "'People Don't Have to Be Aesthetes in Order to Understand It': The Optical Paintings of Edna Andrade," in Institute of Contemporary Art, *Edna Andrade: Optical Paintings, 1963–1986*, January 18–April 6, 2003, pp. 12–32; and Ingrid Schaffner, "Out of Andrade Experience," in Institute of Contemporary Art, *Edna Andrade: Optical Paintings, 1963–1986*, January 18–April 6, 2003, pp. 36–44.

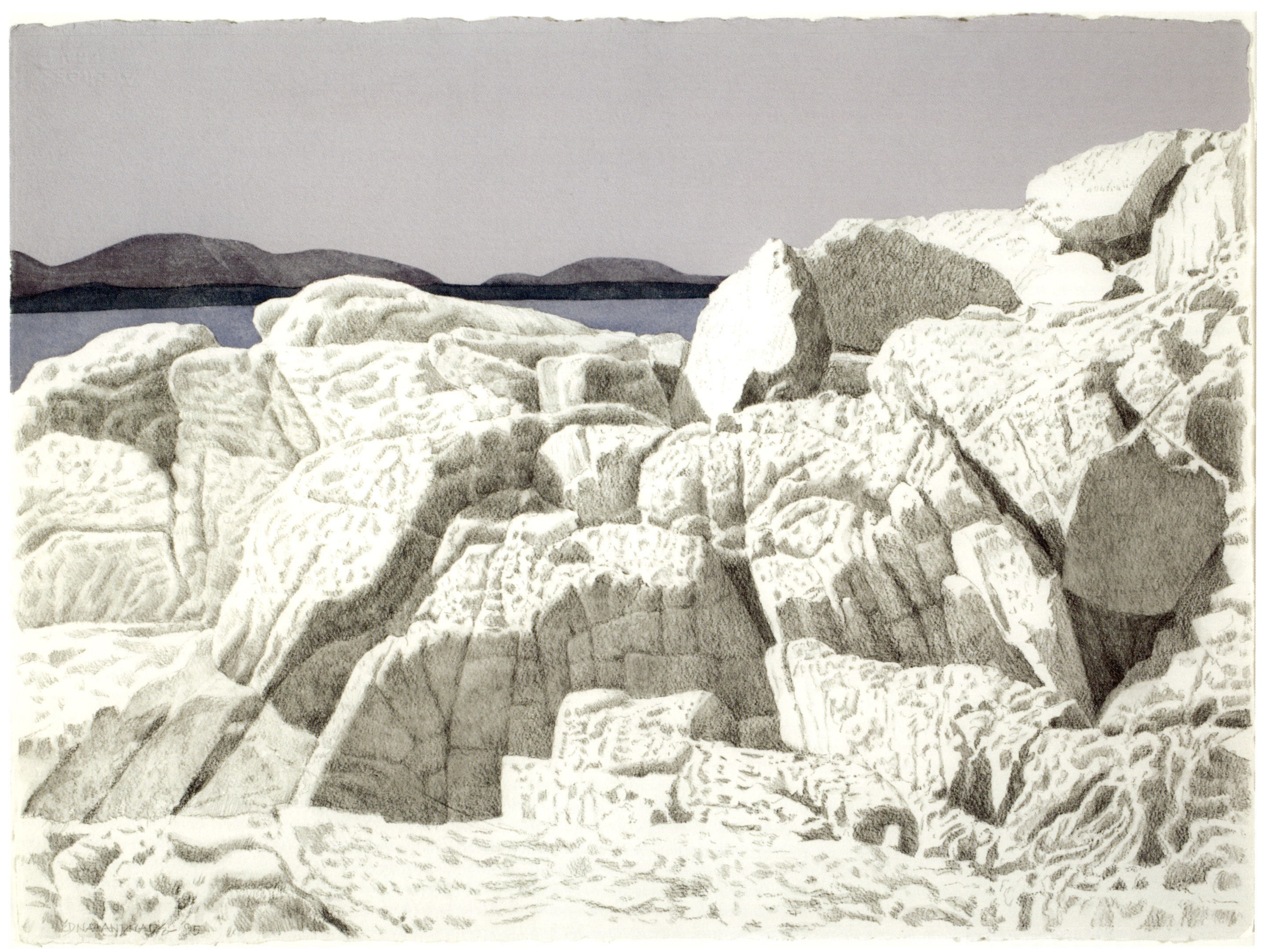

Great Head Toward Mountains, 1995, cat. 46

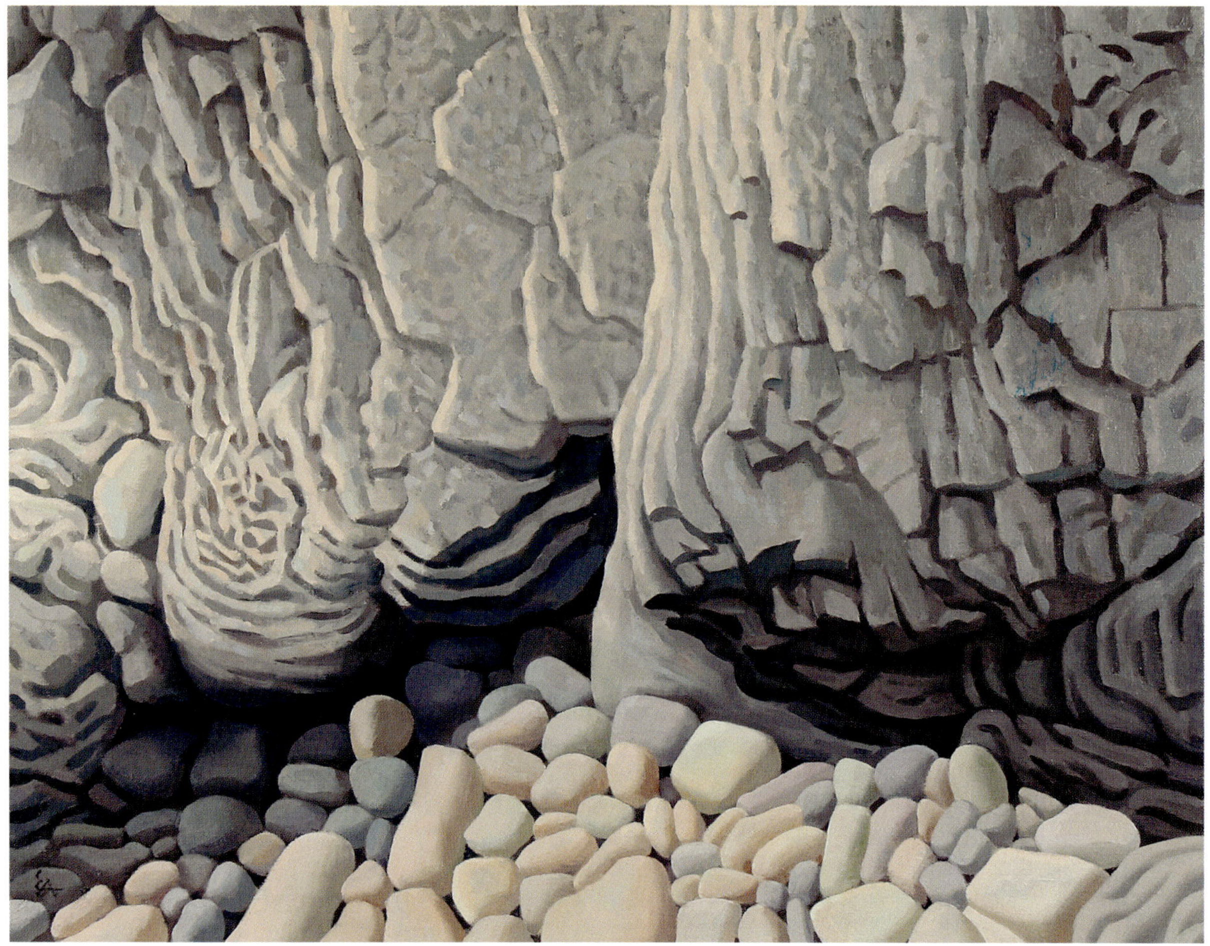

Crevice and Pebbles, 1997–2000, cat. 51

13. Ben Wolf, "Edna Andrade," *The Jewish Exponent*, March 5, 1965, p. 11, quoted in Balken, "People," p. 16.

14. Balken, "People," pp. 21 and 24.

15. Edna Andrade, artist's statement, quoted in a catalogue entry by Anne d'Harnoncourt in Philadelphia Museum of Art, *Philadelphia: Three Centuries of American Art*, April 11–October 10, 1976, p. 637. The impact of feminism in the 1970s is discussed in Schaffner, "Out of Andrade," pp. 40 and 42.

16. Schaffner, "Out of Andrade," p. 40.

17. Wolf, "Edna Andrade," p. 11, quoted in Balken, "People," p. 21.

18. Anne d'Harnoncourt, catalogue entry in Philadelphia Museum of Art, *Philadelphia: Three Centuries*, p. 637; Victoria Donohoe, review in *The Philadelphia Inquirer*, May 8, 1974, quoted in Marian Locks Gallery, *Edna Andrade*, May 2–28, 1977, p. 3; Nessa Forman, review in *The [Philadelphia] Sunday Bulletin*, May 12, 1974, quoted in Marian Locks Gallery, *Edna Andrade*, May 2–28, 1977, p. 3; and Nessa Forman, "Edna Andrade at Locks: Her Sonnets to Life Are Witty and Wise," *The [Philadelphia] Sunday Bulletin*, May 15, 1977.

19. "Andrade regards her work as tackling some 'unfinished 19th-century business.'" Judith Stein, "Edna Andrade at Marian Locks," *Art in America*, vol. 62, no. 5 (September–October 1974), p. 115. Ralph Waldo Emerson's philosophy of Transcendentalism — a seeking, through intuition, of a spiritual state transcending physical phenomena — has long been considered the ideological backbone of the Hudson River School aesthetic of American landscape painting, just as the Sublime — an awe at beholding the infinite — is associated with the paintings of J.M.W. Turner in Britain. Ironically, the Sublime was also a quality attributed to the most ambitious Abstract Expressionist paintings that Andrade's geometric style initially repudiated.

20. Edna Andrade, quoted in Julia Rubalevskaya, "Art Exhibit Gets Rave Reviews," *The [University of Pennsylvania] Daily Pennsylvanian*, January 21, 2003.

21. Edna Andrade, quoted in Debra Bricker Balken, "Edna Andrade," in Locks Gallery, *Edna Andrade: Paintings 1960–1990s*, March 1–29, 1997, p. 4.

22. Edna Andrade, quoted in Rubalevskaya, "Art Exhibit."

23. Edna Andrade, quoted in Wolf, "Edna Andrade," p. 11, quoted in Balken, "People," p. 14.

24. Edna Andrade, artist's statement prepared on June 3, 1971, for the *Exhibition of Geometric Painting by American Artists*, collection of the artist.

25. Edna Andrade, letter to Mildred Staib, March 26, 1983, Woodmere Art Museum Archives.

26. Ann Sutherland Harris, "Cool Waves and Hot Blocks: The Art of Edna Andrade," in Pennsylvania Academy of the Fine Arts, *Cool Waves and Hot Blocks: The Art of Edna Andrade*, September 18, 1993–January 31, 1994, p. 9.

27. Quinn, "Driven to Abstraction," p. 47.

Checklist of the Exhibition

For all dimensions, height precedes width.

1. *Balancing Act*, 1950, oil on masonite, $24\frac{1}{4}$ x $16\frac{1}{2}$ inches, collection of Mrs. Nida Bernstein and Todd Bernstein

2. *Bailey Island*, 1952, ink on gessoed board, 17 x $24\frac{1}{8}$ inches, courtesy of the artist and Locks Gallery

3. *Black Rocks*, 1953, watercolor on board, 22 x 30 inches, Art by Women Collection of Linda Lee Alter

4. *Breaking Wave*, 1953, watercolor on paper, 12 x 18 inches, courtesy of the artist and Locks Gallery

5. *Distant White Boulder*, 1953, charcoal and pastel on tan paper, 12 x 18 inches, courtesy of the artist and Locks Gallery

6. *Pinnacles*, 1953, gouache on green paper, 20 x $26\frac{1}{8}$ inches, courtesy of the artist and Locks Gallery

7. *White Boulder*, 1953, charcoal and pastel on tan paper, 12 x 18 inches, courtesy of the artist and Locks Gallery

8. *Flight of Gulls*, 1958, oil on canvas, 52 x 32 inches, courtesy of the artist and Locks Gallery

9. *Moon Rise*, 1961, ink on paper, $25\frac{1}{8}$ x $32\frac{5}{8}$ inches, collection of Elizabeth Osborne

10. *Dark Figures*, 1962, collage on board, $59\frac{15}{16}$ x 24 inches, courtesy of the artist and Locks Gallery

11. *Garden Dance*, 1962, watercolor on paper, $12\frac{3}{16}$ x $16\frac{1}{8}$ inches, courtesy of the artist and Locks Gallery

12. *Cross*, 1962, oil on canvas, 40 x 36 inches, courtesy of the artist and Locks Gallery

13. *Space Frame Study*, 1965, gouache on board, $7\frac{3}{4}$ x $27\frac{3}{16}$ inches, courtesy of the artist and Locks Gallery

14. *Space Frame D*, 1966–67, oil on canvas, 50 x $50\frac{1}{8}$ inches, Pennsylvania Academy of the Fine Arts, Philadelphia, John Lambert Purchase Fund

15. *Ahmet Hello*, 1967, oil on linen, 24 x 36 inches, courtesy of the artist and Locks Gallery

16. *White Dragons*, 1968, acrylic on board, 29 x 29 inches, courtesy of the artist and Locks Gallery

17. *Criss-Cross*, 1970, inscribed plexiglas, 29 x 29 inches, courtesy of the artist and Locks Gallery

18. *Intersection*, 1970, ink and silver gilt on paper, $19\frac{3}{4}$ x $19\frac{3}{4}$ inches, courtesy of the artist and Locks Gallery

19. *Penta*, 1970, ink wash on paper, 20 x 20 inches, courtesy of the artist and Locks Gallery

20. *Space Dream – Study*, 1972, ink on tracing paper, 5 x 5 inches, collection of Luther W. Brady

21. *Torsion*, 1973, acrylic on canvas, 40 x 40 inches, courtesy of the artist and Locks Gallery

22. *Tensor*, 1975, acrylic on canvas, 66 x 22 inches, courtesy of the artist and Locks Gallery

23. *Drawing 10/6/76*, 1976, graphite and acrylic on paper, $22\frac{1}{4}$ x $29\frac{3}{4}$ inches, courtesy of the artist and Locks Gallery

24. *Untitled*, 1976, graphite and acrylic on paper, $22\frac{3}{4}$ x $30\frac{1}{4}$ inches, Woodmere Art Museum, Gift of Donna Turner Petersen and Robert E. A. Petersen, 1995

25. *Gray Lake*, 1976, acrylic on canvas, 20 x 20 inches, collection of Diane Burko and Richard Ryan

26. *Cascade*, 1978, graphite and silver foil on board, 29 x 29 inches, collection of Michael Basta

27. *Cones, Pyramids, and Prisms*, 1978, colored pencil on paper, $21\frac{3}{4}$ x $29\frac{7}{8}$ inches, collection of Thomas A. Bershad

28. *White Objects with Orange*, 1978, colored pencil on paper, 22 x 30 inches, collection of Essie and Steve Springer

29. *Study for "Crescendo,"* 1979, acrylic on paper, 30 x 24 inches, courtesy of the artist and Locks Gallery

30. *Study for "Fanfare,"* 1979, acrylic on paper, 24 x 30 inches, courtesy of the artist and Locks Gallery

31. *Untitled*, 1980, acrylic on canvas, 42 x 42 inches, courtesy of the artist and Locks Gallery

32. *Arizona Celebration*, 1981, collage on board, 20 x 20 inches, collection of Mr. and Mrs. James B. Straw

33. *Painted Desert Blue*, 1983, collage, 10 x 10 inches, collection of Julie and Neil Courtney

34. *Moon Rise I*, 1983, colored pencil on paper, 14 x 14 inches, collection of Jessica Burko

35. *Moon Rise*, 1983, acrylic on canvas, 30 x 30 inches, Woodmere Art Museum, gift of Donna Turner Petersen and Robert E. A. Petersen, 1995

36. *Pyramid on Gold*, 1984, acrylic on gold board, $5^{11}/_{16}$ x $13^{15}/_{16}$ inches, courtesy of the artist and Locks Gallery

37. *Indian Storm*, 1984, acrylic on paper, $13^{1}/_{2}$ x $13^{1}/_{2}$ inches, Bryn Mawr College Collections, The William and Uytendale Scott Memorial Study Collection, Gift of Bill Scott

38. *Arabian Sea*, 1984, colored pencil and acrylic on black paper, 21 x 13 inches, collection of Ann and Donald McPhail

39. *Reflections*, 1987, collage, $16^{3}/_{8}$ x $16^{3}/_{8}$ inches, collection of Dr. Janice T. Gordon

40. *Windy Sky*, 1988, collage, 10 x 13 inches, collection of Ann and Donald McPhail

41. *Astrologer's Garden*, 1988, collage and acrylic on canvas, 10 x 42 inches, courtesy of the artist and Locks Gallery

42. *Requiem*, 1991, acrylic on mulberry paper collaged on paper, $29^{1}/_{4}$ x $41^{1}/_{4}$ inches, collection of Theodore and Nancie Burkett

43. *Pink Morning*, 1991, acrylic, watercolor, and wax rubbing on mulberry paper collaged on paper, $26^{1}/_{2}$ x 34 inches, courtesy of the artist and Locks Gallery

44. *Triptych Acadia*, 1992, collage on paper, $29^{1}/_{4}$ x $41^{1}/_{4}$ inches, courtesy of the artist and Locks Gallery

45. *Moonlight*, 1992, acrylic, watercolor, and wax rubbing on mulberry paper collaged on paper, $30^{1}/_{4}$ x $40^{1}/_{4}$ inches, collection of Ann and Donald McPhail

46. *Great Head Toward Mountains*, 1995, graphite, acrylic, and watercolor on paper, $22^{7}/_{8}$ x $30^{1}/_{4}$ inches, private collection

47. *Crevice*, 1995, graphite on paper, $22^{3}/_{4}$ x $30^{1}/_{4}$ inches, Art by Women Collection of Linda Lee Alter

48. *Cliff and Cobbles*, 1995, acrylic and graphite on paper, $22^{7}/_{8}$ x $30^{1}/_{2}$ inches, courtesy of the artist and Locks Gallery

49. *Evening Shore*, 1996, graphite and watercolor on paper, $9^{15}/_{16}$ x 15 inches, courtesy of the artist and Locks Gallery

50. *Ledge with Sphere*, 1996, graphite on paper, $29^{1}/_{2}$ x $41^{1}/_{4}$ inches, courtesy of the artist and Locks Gallery

51. *Crevice and Pebbles*, 1997–2000, oil on canvas, 19 x $24^{1}/_{8}$ inches, courtesy of the artist and Locks Gallery

52. *Barrier 7-15-98*, 1998, graphite on paper, 32 x $47^{1}/_{4}$ inches, collection of Dr. Janice T. Gordon

53. *Rocky Head*, 1999, watercolor on paper, $12^{1}/_{8}$ x $16^{1}/_{16}$ inches, courtesy of the artist and Locks Gallery

54. *Back Shore,* 1999–2000, graphite on oil ground on canvas, 30 x 40 inches, courtesy of the artist and Locks Gallery

55. *Cliff Face*, 2000, graphite aquarelle pencil on canvas, 51 x $13^{1}/_{16}$ inches, collection of Portia Sperr

56. *Haze Over Great Head*, 2000–2002, oil on canvas, $30^{1}/_{16}$ x 40 inches, courtesy of the artist and Locks Gallery

57. *Pinnacle,* 2001–2002, graphite on acrylic-primed canvas, $72^{1}/_{2}$ x $42^{1}/_{2}$ inches, courtesy of the artist and Locks Gallery

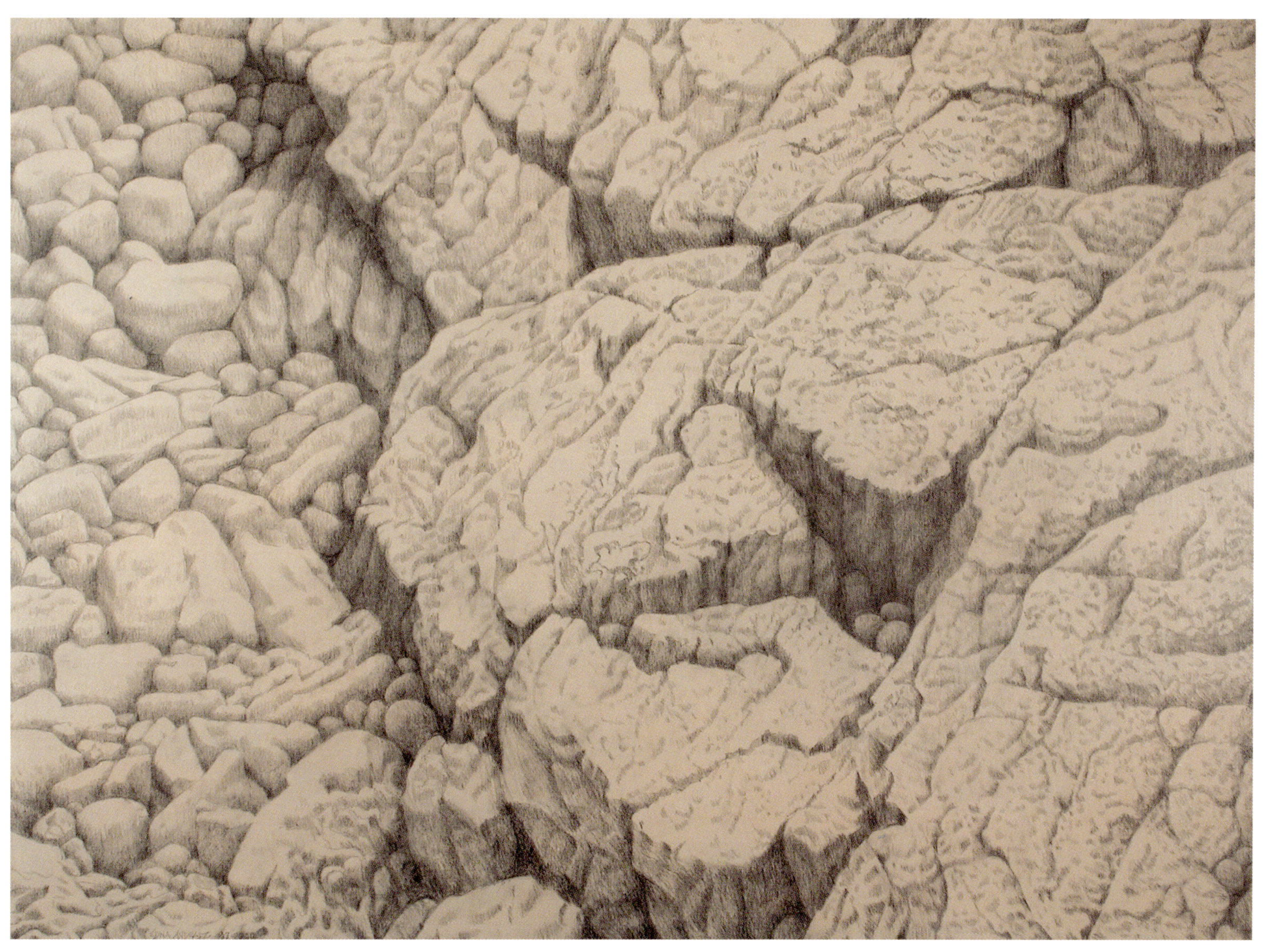

Back Shore, 1999–2000, cat. 54

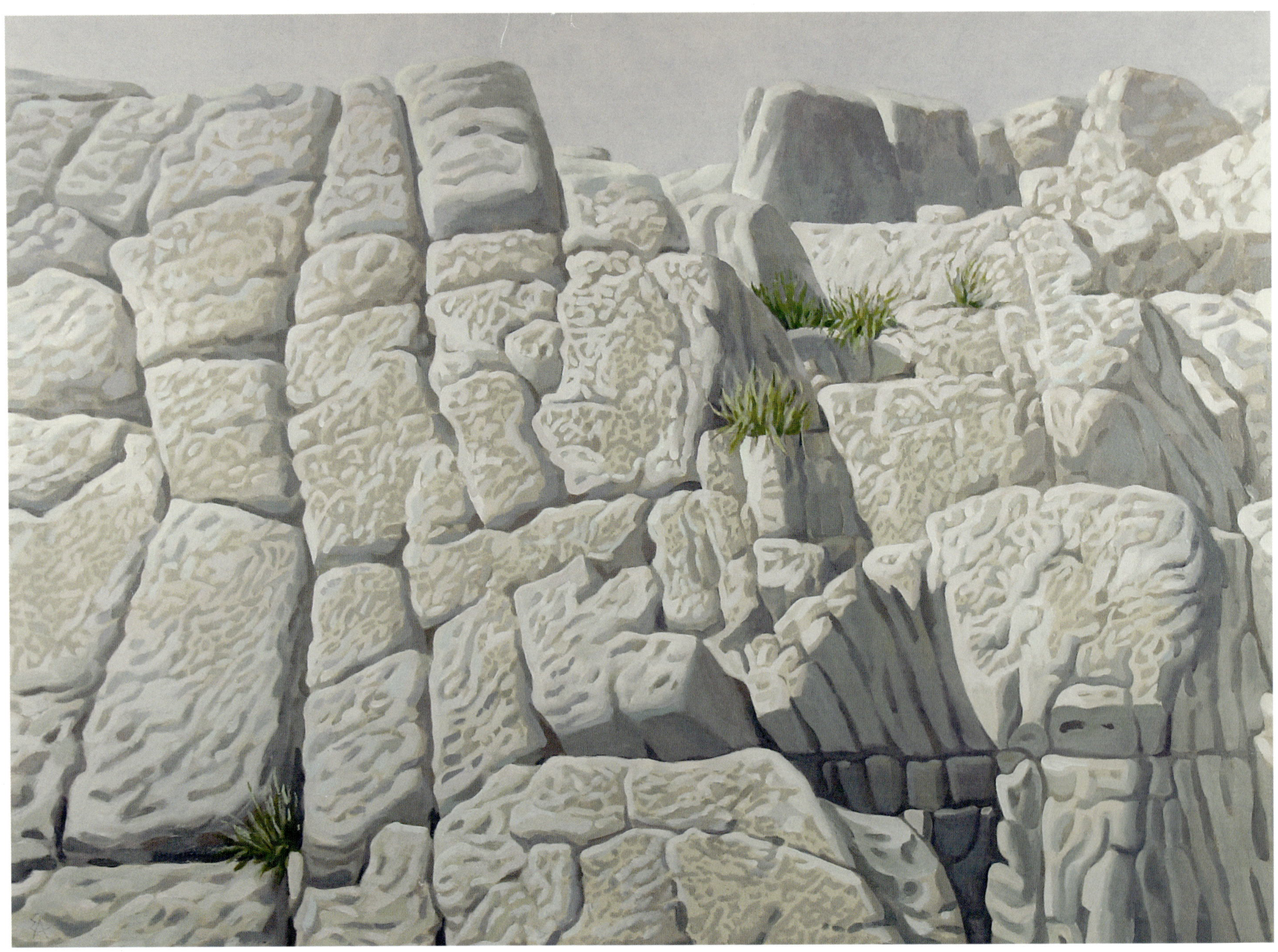

Haze Over Great Head, 2000–2002, cat. 56